Stan Toler's Practical Guide to Leading Staff

How to Empower Your Team and Multiply Ministry

Stan Toler

Indianapolis, Indiana

Published by Wesleyan Publishing House
Indianapolis, Indiana 46250
Printed in the United States of America
ISBN: 978-0-89827-597-1

Library of Congress Cataloging-in-Publication Data

Toler, Stan.
Stan Toler's practical guide to leading staff : how to empower your team and multiply ministry / Stan Toler.
p. cm.
Includes bibliographical references (p.).
ISBN 978-0-89827-597-1
1. Christian leadership. 2. Church management. 3. Pastoral theology. I. Title. II. Title: Practical guide to leading staff.
BV652.1.T655 2012
253'.7--dc23
2012010612

To Wren, my first and most beautiful granddaughter.
May all your dreams come true.

Contents

PREFACE

Few things are more rewarding in pastoral ministry than having the opportunity to lead a ministry staff; yet few pastors feel adequately prepared for the opportunity when it comes. And being an experienced, effective solo pastor is no guarantee that you will find it natural or easy to lead others in having an effective ministry. That's why I've written this book—to lead you step by step through some of the key leadership skills you'll need to learn when you begin to lead staff.

Leading a staff—even a volunteer one—is a whole different ballgame compared to solo ministry. It requires a new set of attitudes and aptitudes. The great thing is that no matter your past experience or lack thereof, these are attitudes and aptitudes that can be learned. As with the previous four books in this series, my goal is to give you both the big ideas and the nuts-and-bolts tools you need to lead your ministry staff effectively.

My aim is to walk with you through both the excitement and the uncertainty and to help equip you to lead your staff with confidence and excellence. Together we can do it!

STAN TOLER

ACKNOWLEDGEMENTS

Many thanks to the team at Wesleyan Publishing House, especially Don Cady, Craig Bubeck, Kevin Scott, Joe Jackson, Rachael Stevenson, and Lyn Rayn. Thanks also to Ron McClung for valuable editorial assistance. Thank you for helping me elevate this project to a new level.

1

Character
Leading Yourself First

Pastors who would lead others successfully must first learn to lead themselves.

In reading the lives of great men, I found that the first victory they won was over themselves. . . . Self-discipline with all of them came first.
—Harry S. Truman

Michael Plant launched his midsized sailboat, the *Coyote*, into the waters of the Atlantic in the autumn of 1992, beginning a solo voyage from the United States to France. Eleven days later, all radio contact went silent.

Nobody was too concerned at first. Plant was an expert sailor. The sailing community considered his skills to be without equal. Besides, his sailboat was state of the art. In addition, he had installed a brand-new, emergency, position-indicating radio beacon—capable of transmitting a signal to a satellite in case of difficulty. Four short bursts from his radio would be enough to determine his location.

Such a signal never came. Ground stations in Canada and the United States picked up a signal of three bursts from a radio like the one mounted in Plant's boat. However, technicians chose to ignore it, since there were only three bursts instead of the required four.

The crew of a freighter eventually found the *Coyote*, floating upside down, 450 miles northwest of the Azores Islands. Plant was not on board and was never found.

To add to the mystery, an eight-thousand-pound weight that had been fastened to the bottom of the sailboat was missing. Such a weight was crucial to keeping the boat upright during a storm or rough seas. Normally, a sailboat never capsizes because builders assure there is greater weight below the waterline than above it.

What happened to the *Coyote*? Why was the weight missing? No one knows.[1]

D. L. Moody reportedly said, "Character is what you are in the dark."[2] Or, I might add, character is what you are below the waterline. Anyone can put on a good front and present an attractive exterior to a casual observer. A person of character possesses qualities that go deeper than outward appearances.

Some pastors never learn to lead others because they have not first learned to lead themselves. To lead yourself requires self-discipline, one of the major components of an upright character. Unfortunately, many have never cultivated what no one can see, what exists below the waterline.

The Challenge of Leading Yourself

How does that relate to leading staff? Unless senior pastors develop their character and learn to lead themselves first, they will not ultimately be successful in leading staff. A potential senior pastor may look at the opportunity to lead a church that is large enough to hire staff and see only the prestige of being a "senior" pastor instead of a solo pastor. Instead, senior pastors must be aware of the challenges, even obstacles, in leading others.

It requires self-discipline. I have a love-hate relationship with self-discipline. I dislike having to watch my weight, which is always a struggle. I dislike many other things that I have to force myself to do. But I love what it accomplishes. An undisciplined life, on the other hand, is like a river that has overflowed its banks.

Our first and greatest challenge is to lead ourselves. Peter the Great ruled Russia and later the Russian Empire from 1682 until 1725. His name officially was Peter I, but he dubbed himself Peter the Great. Still he admitted, "I have conquered an empire, but I have not been able to conquer myself."[3]

Why is it difficult to lead ourselves?

It Is Easier to Lead Others

Many would-be leaders foolishly think all they have to do is give orders and tell others what to do. Then they can sit back and hold someone else responsible when things don't work out the way they're supposed to. Yet that strategy will only work temporarily. Sooner or later, someone begins to think that perhaps the leader of the organization should be held accountable as well as the subordinates he or she has inadequately supervised.

Blessed is the man or woman who understands the power we have to make a difference in our own lives. Some leaders have real power, and others have only the illusion of power. They delude themselves into thinking they have power because they sit in the chair behind the executive desk. Real power comes through influencing others. The most important influence is setting the example of self-discipline and being a person of sterling character.

It Is Difficult to See Yourself with Objectivity

Even looking into a mirror does not guarantee objectivity because we're seeing a reverse image of ourselves. The Scottish poet Robert Burns, in his poem "To a Louse," said (translated from his original Scottish dialect), "O would some Power the gift to give us / To see ourselves as others see us!"[4]

But, alas, most of us don't see ourselves as others see us. We see ourselves through subjective lenses. Thus, it is nearly impossible to discipline what we do not realize needs to be changed.

It Is Difficult to Change Yourself

Even if we become aware of things about ourselves that we need to change, it is difficult to do it. The biggest obstacle to forming a new habit is the old habit. It's comfortable and familiar, and we find it hard to let it go.

I read that the US standard railroad gauge (the distance between the rails) is four feet, eight-and-one-half inches. That is a very odd number. Yet that's the way people built them in England and later in America. The British built them that way because the tramways used that gauge. Tramway builders used that measurement because it was the standard gauge for wagons. Wagons were constructed that way because otherwise the wheels would not match the ruts in the roads. The Romans built the first long-distance roads in Europe. Those first ruts were carved into the earth by Roman war chariots, and the chariots were built that way to accommodate the rear ends of two warhorses![5]

Unfortunately, we often find it hard to change simply because we've always done something one way. Or we have always thought of ourselves the same way. Maybe we don't even know why we think that way; it's just the way it has always been.

It Is Easier to Coast

The truth is, it's easier to coast than it is to change. Disciplining oneself does not happen without a good deal of intentionality. Maybe we should pray the prayer of Samuel Logan Brengle, the renowned preacher of the Salvation Army, who prayed (according to his diary): "Keep me, O Lord, from waxing mentally and spiritually dull and stupid. Help me to keep the physical, mental, and spiritual fiber of the athlete, of the man who denies himself daily and takes up his cross and follows Thee. Give me good success in my work, but hide pride from me. Save me from the self-complacency that so frequently accompanies success and prosperity. Save me from the spirit of sloth, of self-indulgence, as physical infirmities and decay creep upon me."[6]

Such a prayer—and maintaining such an attitude—would go a long way toward helping us resist the temptation to coast instead of changing for the better.

Lack of Self-Leadership Leads to Regret

Harry Emerson Fosdick, renowned preacher of another era, frequently referred to the Great Wall of China. He pointed out that the wall seemed to guarantee no foreign power would ever invade China. Yet the wall did not protect the Chinese. There was nothing wrong with the wall. The problem was with the guards who had a weakness for bribery. Fosdick said, "It was the human element that failed. What collapsed was character which proved insufficient to make the great structure men had fashioned really work."[7]

Always Do Right

Always do right! This will gratify some people and astonish the rest.

—Mark Twain

The only thing that guards our souls from the sinister invaders that would strip our character of its genuineness is Spirit-filled self-discipline.

Biblical Examples of Character

When the prophet Samuel anointed young Saul as Israel's first king, he stood full of promise and possibilities. He was "an impressive young man without equal among the Israelites—a head taller than any of the others" (1 Sam. 9:2). When Samuel first met Saul, he said, "To whom is all the desire of Israel turned, if not to you and all your father's family?" (1 Sam. 9:20). He was implying that the people wanted Saul as king.

Saul's Shallowness

Saul responded, "But am I not a Benjamite, from the smallest tribe of Israel, and is not my clan the least of all the clans of the tribe of Benjamin? Why do you say such a thing to me?" (1 Sam. 9:21).

We might be impressed with Saul's humility. Indeed when the time came to anoint him, the people could not find him. They finally located him, hiding among the baggage (1 Sam. 10:22).

However, his humility was short-lived. After becoming king and experiencing an initial flush of success, Saul spiraled downward. Instead of waiting for Samuel to offer the sacrifice to God, Saul became impatient, took matters into his own hands, and offered the sacrifice himself.

Saul had not learned self-discipline. He acted impulsively and assumed a role God did not intend for him to play. It showed that his depth below the waterline was shallow.

David's Heart

When Saul failed so miserably, the prophet Samuel rebuked him and gave him the heart-wrenching verdict: "You acted foolishly. . . . Now your kingdom will not endure." He continued, "The LORD has sought out a man after his own heart and appointed him leader of his people because you have not kept the LORD's command" (1 Sam. 13:13–14).

That man, the one after God's own heart, was David. Unfortunately, David also had his Achilles' heel. Surrendering to lust and adultery, he compounded his sins by ordering the death of an innocent soldier, Uriah, the husband of David's partner in adultery. Like many other leaders, David apparently rationalized that he was above the rules. Yet one of the major differences between Saul and David was that David had a repentant heart. He acknowledged his sin and prayed, "Create in me a pure heart, O God, and renew a steadfast spirit within me" (Ps. 51:10).

In spite of a tragic, but temporary, lapse of self-discipline, David proved to be a person of good character, with reserves of strength and resilience. His heart for God led him to do the right thing ultimately. His many psalms are a testimony to his spirit of worship and desire to walk in obedience to God, resulting in a strong character.

Joseph's Strength of Character

Joseph was a man of great integrity, resilience, and godliness. As a teenager, he unwisely told his brothers about a dream in which sheaves of grain representing them bowed before a single sheaf of grain that represented Joseph. Later, when Joseph's father, Jacob, sent him to see how the brothers were doing, they said, "Here comes that dreamer! . . . Let's kill him . . . and say that a ferocious animal devoured him. Then we'll see what comes of his dreams" (Gen. 37:19–20).

Instead of killing him, they sold him to a caravan of traders bound for Egypt. The traders in turn sold Joseph to Potiphar, one of the Egyptian pharaoh's officials. It was quite a downturn for one who had dreams of grandeur. But "the LORD was with Joseph and he prospered" (Gen. 39:2). Joseph did his part as well, working hard, finding favor in the eyes of Potiphar, and earning his master's trust.

When Potiphar's wife tried to seduce Joseph, he resisted and fled even though it cost him his position. When Mrs. Potiphar falsely accused the young man, Potiphar had him thrown in prison. Many would have languished in captivity, but Joseph found favor in the eyes of the warden and soon assumed responsibility for everything done in the prison (Gen. 39:22).

Joseph befriended Pharaoh's cupbearer and baker when they landed in prison. Later, after the cupbearer was released and Pharaoh needed someone to interpret his dreams, the cupbearer remembered Joseph and recommended him to the king. Joseph interpreted the ruler's dreams and found favor in his sight. He became second-in-command throughout Egypt and saved the country and others from famine by his careful stewardship of resources.

When his brothers came to Egypt in search of food, Joseph recognized them. With his power and prestige, he could have taken vengeance on them because of the way they had treated him. In fact, when they realized who Joseph was, that is exactly what they thought he would do. Yet Joseph took the high road. He adopted a godly perspective through of all his circumstances and said to his brothers, "You intended to harm me, but God intended it for good to accomplish what is now being done, the saving of many lives" (Gen. 50:20).

Joseph proved that he was a man of great depth. When it came to character, Joseph had significant weight below the waterline. When people have such solid character, they rise to the occasion and lead with grace and truth.

Paul's Self-Discipline

People of solid character resist the danger of complacency. Who could doubt the depth of Paul's character? After all, he testified before kings and governors, before religious and civil authorities, before soldiers and civilians. Yet he understood the importance of self-discipline. He said, "I beat my body and make it my slave so that after I have preached to others, I myself will not be disqualified for the prize" (1 Cor. 9:27).

Of course, Paul did not literally beat his body. There were plenty of others who were only too happy to do that for him. Rather, he disciplined himself to do the right things, say the right things, and keep the right attitudes. He was like the old saint who said to his body, "I go with you three times a day to eat. Now you must come with me to pray!"

Leading Yourself with Authenticity

To be a successful senior pastor and lead others requires that you learn how to lead yourself. As Chris Cree points out, "The military teaches that in order to be a good leader you must first be a good follower. And that is especially true in our society where the military ultimately answers to civilian control. But the principle also applies to life in general."[8]

Here are several principles to guide us in leading ourselves.

Be Honest

Being honest means that you're the same on the inside as you advertise on the outside. Having integrity requires that you are even bigger on the inside.

Before he became president, Theodore Roosevelt was a cowboy in Montana and Wyoming. He once came across one of his ablest cowboys about to brand an unbranded stray. Shocked that the man was going to press the sign of ownership on an animal that obviously did not belong to him, Roosevelt dismissed the man on the spot. The cowboy could not understand why this bespectacled Easterner would treat him so abruptly. Roosevelt explained, "A man who will steal *for* me will steal *from* me. You're fired."[9]

Of all professions, if pastors don't have integrity, they have nothing.

Be Accountable

Across the years, I have seen and heard stories of many pastors who made poor decisions and suffered ethical failures. From adultery to embezzlement to acting as if the lead pastor was above the rules, many ministers have fooled themselves and have done immeasurable damage to the kingdom by their unwise and immoral choices.

John Wesley believed in accountability. He had a small group with whom he met when he was at Oxford University. They met so methodically and lived such disciplined lives that other students ridiculed them and called them "Methodists." That's where the name came from for the denomination that spread so rapidly across the United States in the early years after its organization in Baltimore in 1789.

The problem leaders encounter when they take seriously this matter of leading themselves is just this: We can't trust ourselves.

We are too close to our situations. We "can't see the forest for the trees." This is why we need people who will see us more objectively and hold us accountable.

When President Franklin D. Roosevelt died suddenly early in his fourth term, Harry Truman became president. Speaker of the House Sam Rayburn, a member of Truman's own party, gave him some advice. "From here on out you're going to have lots of people around you. They'll try to put a wall around you and cut you off from any ideas but theirs. They'll tell you what a great man you are, Harry. But you and I both know you ain't."[10] In his own homespun way, Rayburn was holding President Truman accountable.

How American Christians Feel about Accountability

Only 5 percent of self-described Christian adults in the United States say their church holds them accountable for their actions. Among evangelicals, the number rises to 15 percent. Researcher George Barna observes that Americans like their freedom and privacy. So even though mutual accountability is one of the cornerstones of biblical community, many consider being held accountable "inappropriate, antiquated, and rigid."

Live Wisely

Wisdom can be elusive. If you want to live wisely, try practicing common sense. English poet Samuel Taylor Coleridge believed that "common sense in an uncommon degree is what the world calls wisdom."[11]

Living wisely, as it relates to character and self-discipline, is primarily a matter of making good choices. Make good choices regarding how you spend your time. Make good choices in developing relationships. Make good choices in what you read and what you do for entertainment.

"If any of you lacks wisdom, he should ask God, who gives generously to all without finding fault, and it will be given to him" (James 1:5).

Be Generous

When you achieve the status of senior pastor, it usually means you have paid your dues by previously serving in some other capacity. Perhaps you have even served under the leadership of another senior pastor. You may have come into the lead position in a church with a list held tightly in your fist, a list that says, "Things I Will Be Sure to Do (or Not Do) When I Become a Senior Pastor."

Having achieved this point of experience and wisdom in your life, remember to be generous. Share what you know. But don't do it in a condescending way. Do it in a gracious, open-handed way that says, "If I have learned anything helpful, you are welcome to it."

Be an open-handed, open-hearted person who is eager to share what you have learned with others. It says volumes about your character.

Be Kind

We are not equally intelligent. Nor are we equally gifted. But everybody can be kind. This is especially important for the leader because the leader is in the spotlight and what he or she does will influence others.

When Peggy Noonan was writing a book about President Ronald Reagan, she was astonished by all the stories people told her about Reagan. They were almost invariably about his "graciousness, generosity, good humor." The only time she heard a story about his not being kind was when a man told her he had worked in a hotel restaurant one night before Reagan was president, when he came in, stating he had a reservation. They couldn't find his name in the book and the restaurant was full. Because Reagan was famous, they politely asked him to wait a few minutes. However, Reagan lost his temper, berated the man, and left.

The story seemed so out of character for Reagan that Miss Noonan asked the man if he had ever seen Reagan again. He said, "Oh sure, the next morning when he came to apologize."[12]

Kindess

How far you go in life depends on your being tender with the young, compassionate with the aged, sympathetic with the striving and tolerant of the weak and strong. Because someday in life you will have been all of these.

—George Washington Carver

These are all signs of a person of character, a person who has practiced self-discipline, and has learned how to treat other people.

Living It Out

A senior pastor, like people in nearly every profession, has the opportunity to prove his or her character every day. Character is not what the people see on Sunday when we stand in the pulpit. That image may contribute to our reputations. But character is the person we are day in and day out.

Consequently, the senior pastor must pay attention to daily activities, attitudes, and actions. All those things reveal the real person on the inside.

Keep Your Word

Always do what you say you will do. As Brian Tracy points out, "Character is the ability to follow through on a resolution long after the emotion with which it was made has passed."[13]

If you make a promise to a staff member, keep it. If you make a promise to a board member, keep it. If you make a promise to your spouse or child, keep it. If you find it impossible to keep it, apologize and do it with sincerity. Then be careful about future promises.

Don't Run from Adversity

When terrorists flew airplanes into the twin towers of the World Trade Center in New York City on September 11, 2001, thousands of people ran away from the site. But hundreds also ran toward it. They were the first responders, firefighters, police officers, and rescue workers. And hundreds of them gave their lives in the effort.

In a similar way, a pastor reveals character when, instead of running from adversity, he or she turns and faces it. It sets a powerful example for others and reveals a person with depth below the waterline.

What Defines Character

The depth and strength of a human character are defined by its moral reserves. People reveal themselves completely only when they are thrown out of the customary conditions of their life, for only then do they have to fall back on their reserves.

—Leon Trotsky

Instead of running from adversity, we must embrace it when it comes. Phillips Brooks said, "Do not pray for tasks equal to your powers; pray for powers equal to your tasks. Then the doing of your work shall be no miracle, but you shall be a miracle. Every day you shall wonder at yourself, at the richness of life which has come to you by the grace of God."[14]

Know What Is Important

This advice can help us in many ways, but what I am thinking about here is just this: Care about your reputation, but be more concerned about your character. Theodore Roosevelt said, "I care not what others think of what I do, but I care very much about what I think of what I do! That is character!"[15]

I understand what Roosevelt meant, but the truth is, I do care what people think, because that has to do with my reputation. Someone astutely observed that reputation is like fine china: easily cracked and never well-mended. But while I am concerned about reputation, I am even more concerned about character. Reputation is what people think you are. Character is what you really are. Dwight L. Moody said, "If I take care of my character, my reputation will take care of itself."[16]

Always Take Responsibility for Your Actions

When people try to duck responsibility, it reveals a flaw in their character. When we blame others or try to wiggle out of taking responsibility, it shows that we have an internal weakness.

Stephen Covey believes "our character is basically a composite of our habits. Because they are consistent, often unconscious patterns, they constantly, daily, express our character."[17]

Be Persistent

Perhaps you have noticed that people, including yourself, may be strong in one area, but weaker in another. We don't necessarily conquer every flaw at the same time.

Be persistent. If you have not yet ironed out every wrinkle, there is hope. Satan may probe and taunt you at the point of your weakness, but God's grace is sufficient.

What's Below the Waterline

A sailboat with heavy weight below the waterline never capsizes. But a boat that has that weight missing is easy prey for every wave that comes.

Finding Leaders of Good Character

Although this chapter is about the pastor leading himself, pastors must also look for lay leaders who have character. The apostle Paul urged his protégés to choose leaders of good character: "Those who have served well gain an excellent standing and great assurance in their faith in Christ Jesus" (1 Tim. 3:13).

The same is true of people. When adversity or a particularly heavy temptation comes—and it always does—your integrity can remain intact if you are a person of solid character. Not to be morbid, but when you come to the end of your life, after someone says a few words over your cold, silent form, the funeral director will close the lid on your casket. That is when "the only thing that walks back from the tomb with the mourners and refuses to be buried is the character of a man. This is true. What a man is survives him. It can never be buried."[18]

Only pastors who have developed the ability to discipline themselves will achieve depth of character.

Action Steps

1. Form an accountability group if you don't already have one.
2. How do your choices of reading material and leisure time activities reflect on your character?
3. Make a list of the people with whom you have spent the most time in the past month. How have they provided stimulus to or detraction from your character development?

2

CULTURE
IDENTIFYING VALUES AND EXPECTATIONS

You and your staff need to understand your church's values and expectations.

It's not hard to make decisions when you know what your values are.
—ROY DISNEY, WALT'S BROTHER AND PARTNER

A church of several hundred attendees went through a pastoral change. Within the first three months of the new minister's tenure, he changed the worship style. He dismissed the choir director and the choir of sixty voices. The new style was contemporary and people were expected to like it. Instead, they began to leave in droves.

A general superintendent knew I was a friend of the pastor and asked me if I would speak to him about the direction the church was taking. As a fellow pastor, I had no authority over my colleague, but the superintendent thought that because of our friendship, I might be persuasive.

Reluctantly, I called him and set up a luncheon appointment. Over our meal, I asked if he had considered options. Instead of changing everything, maybe he could offer a contemporary service as well as retaining the choir and a more traditional approach in a different service.

He said, "You are probably right, but I do not have a reverse gear." He could not bring himself to admit, "I moved too hastily. Let's restore some of the things we changed and offer options." To be sure, it was an ego problem, but it was also a breach of the congregation's culture without due regard for many people who had invested their time, money, and energy to build the church.

Over time, the church's attendance spiraled down until fewer than a hundred people were attending. It was a shadow of its former self. Some of the changes the pastor made were good and probably needed to be made. But he implemented them too quickly. The pastor's indifference to the church's culture has left a diminished congregation that may never recover its former vitality.

The Variety of Expectations

David McKenna told about a pastor who moved into a large metropolitan church known for its Scandinavian origins. Here he met people with last names like Johnson, Anderson, and Swanson. His own name revealed Welsh roots, which he felt put him at a disadvantage in relating to his new parishioners. At the same time, he knew little about their Scandinavian customs.

Observers outside the parish did not give the pastor much chance of survival. But when McKenna visited him, the pastor told about one of his earliest encounters with the culture. A committee wanted to paint the recreation area with strong, bold colors of blue and yellow. The pastor started to object but then remembered that these are the colors in the Swedish flag. Wisely, he said nothing and agreed with their decision. McKenna concluded, "When I heard him tell the story I felt sure that he would survive to serve. He has."[1]

Every church has its unique culture. Some have contemporary worship styles; others are traditional, and some have succeeded in achieving a blend that works for most people. Some churches are blue collar in their makeup while others are primarily white collar. Some are urban while others are suburban or rural. Some churches are affluent while others are poor or middle class. Some churches are homogeneous. That is, everybody looks and acts pretty much the same. Others are diverse, with a multiethnic, multicultural, or multigenerational flavor.

Some churches are quite evangelistic; others place a strong emphasis on discipleship. Some are conservative while others are liberal. Some are missional and are successful in reaching out to the community, but others are in maintenance mode, isolated and ingrown. Some are charismatic, while other are reserved. Some churches are youth-oriented and others appeal to older people.

Some churches are so organized they have protocols for everything imaginable. Others lack discernible organization. One man said, "I don't like organized religion." His friend answered, "You'd love our church. We're not very organized at all!"

Values and Expectations

With every church's culture comes a set of values and expectations. When pastors first arrive at a church and begin their ministry, they have a window of leniency. That is, people will understand if the pastor makes small breaches of protocol in the way things are done; but that window will soon close. After that, if the pastor violates protocol, the consequences will be more serious.

Marshall Shelley listed nine separate functions that churches often expect a senior pastor to fulfill: (1) servant-shepherd;

(2) prophet-politician; (3) preacher-enthraller; (4) teacher-theologian; (5) evangelist-exhorter; (6) organizer-promoter; (7) caller-comforter; (8) counselor-reconciler; and (9) equipper-enabler.[2] Is anybody confused yet?

High Expectations

Don't join an easy crowd; you won't grow. Go where the expectations and the demands to perform are high.
—Jim Rohn

In one classic case, the pastor attended his first board meeting after assuming leadership of a church. He pointed out to the board that the lawn was looking a bit shaggy and needed to be mowed. A member responded that the former pastor always mowed the lawn. The new pastor said, "Yes, but I talked to him and he doesn't want to do it anymore!"

Sometimes the expectations have little to do with the job. Onlookers scrutinize the pastor's family and pass judgment on his or her parenting skills. They may think the pastor's car is too old and reflects poorly on what the church pays. On the other hand, if it's too new, they become jealous and wish they could drive such a nice vehicle. Or there may be unwritten expectations for the pastor's spouse.

Staff Pastors Not Exempt

Staff pastors are subject to such scrutiny as well. Conflicting expectations may rule the day, such as expecting professional performance from the worship team but expressing displeasure if the rehearsals are too long or demanding. A youth pastor may be expected to spend time with the teens at every opportunity, yet be available in the office if anyone calls.

In the face of such potential confusion, staff members may need a tutorial on "the way things are done" at that church. For instance, youth pastors who have grown up in urban settings all their lives and move into a rural setting may need a few pointers about expectations in a farming community. A minister of outreach whose experience has been in rural settings will need to understand expectations are different in an urban or suburban congregation.

A colleague told me about inviting a promising young man who had grown up in the South to visit the senior pastor's church in the North, with the idea of possibly coming as youth pastor. After a weekend visit, the young man shook hands with the pastor and informed him that he would not be pursuing the matter further. The reason? The young man was married with no children, but he had decided he did not want to rear his children as Yankees. The culture of the Northern church did not fit his Southern upbringing. The differences in regional culture were too great for him to imagine overcoming.

Core Values

When Jim Collins did the research for his best-selling book *Good to Great*, he found that great companies have core values. In fact, they are "essential for enduring greatness, but it doesn't seem to matter what those core values are." For a local church, however, the core values must fit the Great Commission and the Great Commandment. You can't build a great church on shallow core values.

What plagues many staff members are the expectations that come with a job—expectations which may be unrealistic and over which they have little control. It's a case of heavy stress over unrealistic demands with no opportunity to give input about the outcome!

Taking Bad Advice

Isaiah declared that God exceeded humankind's expectations: "When you came down long ago, you did awesome deeds beyond our highest expectations. And oh, how the mountains quaked!" (Isa. 64:3 NLT).

But you and I are not God, and our performance sometimes falls short of other people's expectations. Blessed is the man or woman who occasionally exceeds people's expectations. By God's grace, he does sometimes enable us to perform "above and beyond." But in many situations, trying to fulfill expectations is a minefield of disastrous possibilities.

Rehoboam's Folly

Rehoboam did not even try. When he took over the kingdom of Israel from his father, Solomon, the nation had risen to great heights. It was a golden age. Yet it came at a great price. Solomon had expensive tastes which resulted in heavy taxes on the people. So Jeroboam, brother to the new king, came to Rehoboam with a delegation of the people. "Your father put a heavy yoke on us," they said, "but now lighten the harsh labor and the heavy yoke he put on us, and we will serve you" (1 Kings 12:4).

The novice king told them to leave for three days and then come back for his answer. Meanwhile, he consulted the elders who had served his father, Solomon. He asked how they would advise him. They said, "If today you will be a servant to the people and serve them and give them a favorable answer, they will always be your servants" (1 Kings 12:7).

Their answer was not what the king wanted to hear so he turned to the young men who had grown up with him. He asked for their advice and they said he should tell the people, "My little finger is thicker than my father's waist. My father laid on you a heavy yoke; I will make it even heavier. My father scourged you with whips; I will scourge you with scorpions" (1 Kings 12:10–11).

Having read the story, we know whose advice Rehoboam took. But we want to scream, "Listen to your father's advisers! They are wise men. Taking the young men's advice will lead to disaster." We can see the storm clouds of rebellion gathering on the horizon. We know that when Rehoboam gave the wrong answer—the harsh answer—disaster would overtake his kingdom.

The new king was foolish. When Jeroboam and the people returned, the king, who did not have the wisdom Solomon had in his "little finger," gave them the harsh answer his young colleagues recommended. Consequently, the people rebelled against Rehoboam, the kingdom divided into Israel and Judah, and "there was continual warfare between Rehoboam and Jeroboam" (1 Kings 14:30).

Likewise, the pastor who ignores the values and expectations of the people is likely to face rebellion at some point. The congregation may divide and "warfare" of one kind or another may erupt.

Paul's Method

On the other hand, how do we square this with the experience of the apostle Paul? He said, "Even though I am free of the demands and expectations of everyone, I have voluntarily become a servant to any and all in order to reach a wide range of people: religious, nonreligious, meticulous moralists, loose-living immoralists, the defeated, the demoralized—whoever" (1 Cor. 9:19–20 MSG).

This sounds like a recipe for a nervous breakdown: trying to meet everybody's expectations. Yet Paul shared how he kept his sanity. He said, "I didn't take on their way of life. I kept my bearings in Christ—but I entered their world and tried to experience things from their point of view. I've become just about every sort of servant there is in my attempts to lead those I meet into a God-saved life. I did all this because of the Message. I didn't just want to talk about it; I wanted to be in on it!" (1 Cor. 9:21–23 MSG).

Did you pick up the key? Two things: "I kept my bearings in Christ" and "I did all this because of the Message." Or as another translation puts it, "For the sake of the gospel" (1 Cor. 9:23).

Someone has attributed this quote to Abraham Lincoln: "You can please some of the people all of the time, you can please all of the people some of the time, but you can't please all of the people all of the time."[3] While we can't ignore the expectations of others, we can center our decision-making on Christ and his principles. We can run them through the filter of what he would do. "What would Jesus do?" is more than a trendy slogan. It becomes a filter to help us determine what makes sense and what does not. What is worthwhile and what is foolish? What is a godly approach and what is a selfish one?

The other filter is "for the sake of the gospel." What will help us do the most effective job of communicating the gospel of Christ? How can we reach the most people with the greatest message of all time? Paul's motivation was "to win as many as possible" (1 Cor. 9:19), and that must be our motivation too.

Wisely paying attention to the values and expectations of the congregation and then communicating that culture to staff members will enable a lead pastor to be more effective in the long run.

Managing Expectations

A pitfall into which many pastors have fallen is that of unwritten expectations. How could we possibly write down everything we expect of the congregation or they expect of us? Yet pastors are wise to probe a bit to discover, if possible, what some of those unwritten expectations are. Otherwise, pastors and congregations inevitably clash.

Clashing Expectations

When Pastor Jim accepted the call of the Pleasant Valley Church, he moved to a congregation known for its affluence. The church held a membership at the local country club and one of the perks of the job was that the pastor could enjoy its amenities on a regular basis. Jim's predecessor often ate Sunday lunch there with his family.

Jim came into the new congregation with a heart for the homeless and the immigrants who had recently moved to the city. Although he made that clear in his interview, and the governing board understood the need for outreach to those less fortunate, he and they held widely different expectations about how that ministry would occur. From Jim's viewpoint, membership in the country club communicated the wrong set of values. Expectations clashed almost from the first week he was there.

It is no surprise that expectations between pastor and parishioners sometimes clash. But as Richard P. Hansen points out, "We begin to deal with these expectations by realizing they enter our lives in two quite different ways": externally and internally.[4]

External Expectations

External expectations are those imposed from outside the pastor. They represent all those things that compete for a pastor's time and energy. They may come from community leaders who expect the pastor to be involved in a service club, like Kiwanis or Rotary. Others may anticipate the pastor will take a leading role in other community activities.

Denominational executives have their own expectations of pastors under their supervision. Attendance at training events, inspirational seminars, and denominational meetings can demand significant involvement.

The local ministerial organization may anticipate that the pastor will want to join and make meaningful contributions. The pastor may feel some pressure to serve on the program committee or serve as an officer in the organization.

Of course, the members of one's own church have certain expectations. Many will be offended if the pastor is not available when they feel the need to call.

The pastor's family—often the last to be considered—will have their own expectations. Spouses and children have a way of coming up on the short end of the schedule if the pastor is not proactive in planning time for them.

Internal Expectations

Internal expectations are those that originate within ourselves. As you go about your daily activities, whose expectations are you trying to meet?

A friend of mine took his first pastorate, and his first few sermons sounded like they were prepared for his professors. Fresh from the academic experience, he was still doing research and striving for academic excellence as if he was going to be graded on the outcome. In a way, of course, the congregation does grade our performances and votes with their feet and wallets as to whether they return or put anything in the offering plate.

But in this case, the pastor had a winsome wife who was a great help. The church was small and the pastor operated out of a home office. After writing his sermon, he read part of it to his wife, an elementary education major. When asked for feedback, she told him, "I think I understand what you're saying, but I wonder if you could reword it so the young people could get it too."

He changed his internal expectations from trying to please his professors, who were now a hundred miles away, to communicating effectively to his congregation.

Other pastors try to live up to the standard of some super-pastor. After attending a conference at a megachurch, many pastors have gone home and tried to emulate the super-pastor of that megachurch. Never mind that the pastor's personality and life experience are quite different from the super-pastor. That ultimately becomes a source of frustration.

Other pastors are highly motivated by the books they read. Consequently, the criteria suggested by some authors may become an internal expectation for the pastor. Although no one else expects it, the pastor keeps trying to live up to the expectations expressed in books.

Professors, super-pastors, and books can all provide inspiration and motivation for the pastor. But we need to be careful lest their models and examples lead to unrealistic expectations for our own ministries.

Role Expectations versus Personal Expectations

Role expectations consist of those things that make up the profession, one's occupation as a pastor. Pastors are expected to perform certain duties. Personal expectations consist of things like personality, mannerisms, the way a pastor dresses, and even idiosyncrasies.

I know a pastor who has always been the epitome of professionalism. He always dressed the part, wearing a suit and tie in the pulpit and behaving in a professional manner. Nobody would ever accuse him of being inappropriate in any way.

When he left that congregation, a younger pastor took his place. On his first Sunday he entered the pulpit without a tie. His communication style was informal. He held people's interest, but he did so in a much more conversational tone than his predecessor had used. Instead of standing in the foyer and greeting people afterwards, he stayed near the front of the church and mingled with the people.

It took some time for adjustment, but gradually the congregation came to accept him as fulfilling the pastoral role as effectively as his predecessor even though his personal style was quite different.

Communicating Values

One of the clear responsibilities of a senior pastor is to help staff pastors, especially new ones, understand the values and expectations of the local church. If a congregation is large enough to employ an executive pastor, whose responsibility it is to supervise staff, the senior pastor may be able to delegate this task. Otherwise, it is the senior pastor's job to see that these expectations are clearly communicated.

Develop Clear Job Descriptions

One way to communicate expectations is through a written job description. If a young assistant is hired and is simply told, "Your job is to run the youth program," we should not be surprised if someone says, "Why isn't the church van washed and filled with gas? The former youth pastor saw to it that the van was ready each week."

Ah, but did anyone tell the new staff person about that expectation? I have never yet seen a job description that covers every possible nuance that the job might include. I have seen some that were extremely detailed and ran several pages in length, so that the most courageous youth pastor might be intimidated from the start. Yet, it is wise to make a conscientious effort to spell out the expectations of the job as clearly as possible.

How We Treat Others

In *My Fair Lady*, Eliza Doolittle says to Colonel Pickering, "You see, . . . the difference between a lady and a flower girl is not how she behaves, but how she's treated. I shall always be a flower girl to Professor Higgins, because he always treats me as a flower girl and always will; but I know I can be a lady to you, because you always treat me as a lady and always will." How we treat staff members influences how well they meet our expectations.

Publicize the Job Description

By publicize, I do not mean that the entire community needs to know the job description. But those who must evaluate staff members and make final decisions about their tenure should be well acquainted with the job description. Some churches publicize the job descriptions as a part of the annual report to the congregation. You will have to determine if that is the best policy for your church. At the very least, job descriptions should be known well enough that there is no question whether a staff person is fulfilling formal expectations.

Evaluate on the Basis of the Job Description

When annual performance review time arrives, performance can be compared to the job description. This helps the review to be more objective than simply basing it on a subjective opinion of how the staff member is doing his or her job. It also saves the staff member from the evaluation of a hundred different bosses in the congregation. The wise senior pastor will also take into account the strengths and weaknesses of the staff member and determine if it would be wise to adjust the job description to better fit the staff person's capabilities.

Develop Volunteers

If you happen to be a pastor without a staff and feel you are not meeting people's expectations, maybe it's time to develop some volunteers who can help you accomplish the expectations. If you delegate some of the things you can't do, you run the risk that the person to whom you delegate it will drop the ball. But it's worth the risk in order to free up your schedule so you can focus on the things only you can do.

Develop a Policy Handbook

A policy handbook can save confusion about many things. Who has the right to use church vehicles? Who is responsible for their maintenance? What are parameters for use of the church kitchen? Who assigns the usage of rooms in the church? When a church has multiple staff members, it is wise to spell out clear policies about such things as vacations, sick days, personal days, and working hours and expectations.

Communicate

It has been said so often in church circles that it runs the risk of sounding trite, but there is no substitute for good communication. With all the means available to us now, one would think there is no excuse for poor communication. Yet we somehow manage to misunderstand one another all too often. I would rather be accused of saying something too often than accused of not saying it enough.

Know Yourself

When we know our own weaknesses and strengths, we can make better decisions regarding the kinds of staff persons we need to be hire. A colleague was the pastor of a rapidly growing church in a community where many university students attended. Burgeoning worship attendance was not accompanied by a growing income. The students were wonderful but had little money.

So when the church finally grew to the point it could hire additional staff, the senior pastor wisely chose to hire a minister of assimilation. He was taking care of preaching and administration, but was falling behind on the assimilation of new people. He purposefully sought a people-person because he knew that someone skilled in building relationships with newcomers was vitally important. The person whom he hired was a perfect fit and the church continued to grow. It worked because the senior pastor knew his own strengths and weaknesses.

Endeavor to Live by God's Standard

Senior pastors find out over the course of time that it is not possible to please everyone. There are too many different people with too many expectations to satisfy them all. So leaders must realize that not everyone will be pleased with every decision. Nor will everyone be happy with every staff person's performance.

"Perhaps the whole question of expectations would become academic if we would constantly be monitoring our lives by this standard: 'Does it meet God's expectations?'"[5]

Adding Value

In most churches with multiple staff, it is the senior pastor's job to supervise staff persons. So the senior pastor becomes the key person to be sure staff members understand the values and expectations of a local congregation.

Every local church has its own set of values. They will typically be similar to other evangelical congregations, but don't overlook the local flavor that influences such things. It is easier to work in an organization when you know what the values and expectations are that govern the working relationship.

A value that congregations may not articulate, but will nevertheless think is important when it is violated, is that of doing what is in the best interest of the church. I have read articles relating how executives have told their employees that everything they do must add value to their customers. How could we conscientiously believe and practice anything less for the church of the Lord Jesus Christ?

Action Steps

1. Does every staff person at your church have a clear job description? If not, make that a priority in the weeks to come.
2. How are annual performance reviews handled? Are they based on objective job descriptions or subjective judgments? Work on eliminating any unfair practices.
3. Does your church have a policy handbook? If not, make that a priority. If it does, review it to be sure it is up-to-date.

3

Vision

Discovering the Attainable Dream

Senior pastors must ensure agreement and alignment among staff pastors on a common vision.

If your actions inspire others to dream more, learn more, do more and become more, you are a leader.
—John Quincy Adams

Pastor Tim, the new youth minister, had been at Sunnyvale Church only a few weeks, but attendance was booming. With both charisma and character, he attracted young people by the droves. Teens were inviting teens and young people were showing up in record numbers. The church was pleased that it had accepted the senior pastor's recommendation to hire this bright young man, fresh out of seminary.

One afternoon the pastor stuck his head in the youth pastor's office and said, "Tim, let's go for a ride." They drove a few blocks and the pastor pulled over to the curb. He sat still for a few moments and just stared at the high school across the street. Tim, a bit nervous by the silence, cleared his throat as if he were about to say something. Just then, they heard a school bell ringing in the distance. Within moments, the doors opened and a river of high school students flowed out of the building.

"Tim," the pastor said, "look at the young people streaming out of that school. How many students attend there?"

Tim wasn't sure, but he knew it was several hundred, perhaps as many as fifteen hundred. The senior pastor nodded and then spoke quietly. "And what percentage of them are part of our youth group?"

Even with all his recent success, Tim knew the percentage was small, and he named a conservative figure. The pastor nodded again and said, "Well, it looks like we have our work cut out for us, doesn't it?"

He started the engine and drove back to the church.

Sidetracking Your Vision

Not every vision is attainable. Some people are so misguided in their pronouncements about the future that it's a good thing we don't practice the Old Testament admonition about putting false prophets to death (Deut. 13:1–5; 18:20–22).

For instance, in 1945 Admiral William D. Leahy expressed his opinion about the atomic bomb to President Harry Truman: "That is the biggest fool thing we have ever done. The bomb will never go off, and I speak as an expert in explosives."[1]

Daniel Webster, erudite member of Congress, gave a speech in the US Senate in 1848, in which he said, "I have never heard of anything, and I cannot conceive of anything more ridiculous, more absurd, and more affrontive to all sober judgment than the cry that we are profiting by the acquisition of New Mexico and California. I hold that they are not worth a dollar!"[2]

In 1903 Henry Adams believed humanity had less than a half-century to live. He predicted, "My figures coincide in fixing 1950 as the year when the world must go to smash."[3] A pastor's vision that is truly from God will avoid such wild speculations and negative expectations.

Capturing God's vision for the church is one thing. Communicating it in such a way that it captivates others and motivates them is something else. Yet that is exactly what a senior pastor must do if he or she is to keep the staff focused and moving forward. Like everything else worth doing in life, the way forward is fraught with obstacles.

Poor Relationships

If the pastor does not have a good relationship with his or her staff, they are not likely to hear the pastor's vision with any degree of enthusiasm. If pastors don't have good relationships, they are not likely to motivate others to run with their vision. Good relationships require something called "social intelligence." Authors Carole Hyatt and Linda Gottlieb believe it is possible to "have great academic intelligence and still lack social intelligence—the ability to be a good listener, to be sensitive toward others, to give and take criticism well."[4]

Relationships Matter

Technology does not run an enterprise, relationships do.

—Patricia Fripp

In fact, if your staff members don't like you, don't expect their cooperation. "You can get away with serious mistakes if you are socially intelligent. . . . A mistake may actually *further* [your] career" if your staff thinks you "handled the situation in a mature and responsible way."[5]

Lack of Agenda Harmony

Church planters know that it's important to beware of prospective members who have their own agenda. A new church begins meeting and dissatisfied members of other churches often drift in, looking for an opportunity to begin again with a new face and voice. However, having had experience in their former church, they already know "how it ought to be done." Wise pastors do their best to discover these agendas before embracing a new member who is not really on board with the pastor's vision.

Careful interviews and conscientious reference checking should precede the hiring of any staff, but occasionally a pastor gets "stung" by a staff member whose agenda is different from the pastor's. If the pastor and staff person can come to a meeting of the minds, it may be possible to salvage the relationship and move forward. If it is not possible to bring agendas into harmony, the pastor is better off to encourage the staff member to move on to a situation more in harmony with the direction he or she prefers.

An Unfocused Vision

Sometimes a pastor enunciates his or her vision, but it lacks focus. If a pastor expresses a vision in terms that are too general, vague, or scattered, a perceptive staff person will find it difficult to get excited about the vision. When a vision is unfocused, one's organization is apt to saddle up and ride off in all directions. Consequently, staff members may chase every new idea, causing them to lose energy. A clear vision, on the other hand, tends to energize.

If you sense your vision is unfocused, go back and look at it again, analyzing it critically. Ask yourself questions designed to bring more detail. It may not be necessary to define every point, but you do have to be specific enough that people don't wonder where you are going.

Young People and Their Visions

The Old Testament prophets knew something about vision. They saw literal visions and communicated them to the people, under the inspiration of the Holy Spirit. God gave the prophet Joel a vision in which the Lord said, "I will pour out my Spirit on all people. Your sons and daughters will prophesy, your old men will dream dreams, your young men will see visions. Even on my servants, both men and women, I will pour out my Spirit in those days" (Joel 2:28–29).

Peter said this vision became a reality on the day of Pentecost. Faced with the accusation that those who were filled with the Spirit had indulged in too much wine, Peter said, "No, this is what was spoken by the prophet Joel" (Acts 2:16), and he quoted the passage above.

While God's vision for your church may not be in the same category as the visions God gave the ancient prophets to communicate to the people, there are similarities. The visions from God often painted word pictures for people to understand what would happen in the future. The vision God gives you for your church will likely be some kind of picture that expresses God's preferred future for your congregation.

Writing Down Your Biblical Goal

A vision from God is worth writing down. Habakkuk testified that "the Lord answered me and said, 'Record the vision and inscribe it on tablets, that the one who reads it may run. For the vision is yet for the appointed time; it hastens toward the goal, and it will not fail. Though it tarries, wait for it; for it will certainly come, it will not delay'" (Hab. 2:2–3 NASB).

Fred Smith told about working for Maxey Jarman, who challenged him anytime his thinking was fuzzy. He forced Fred to write him a memo. Once Fred remonstrated and said, "I can't write it."

Jarman answered, "The only reason you can't write it is because you don't know it. When you know it, you can write it."[6] If you don't know it well enough to write it, don't expect your staff to embrace the vision. Ask the Lord to clarify the vision until you can write it, speak it, and live it.

While Scripture is full of examples of good men who received a vision from the Lord and faithfully communicated it, the Bible also warns us about speaking a vision that is not from the Lord. Through the prophet Jeremiah, the Lord said, "Do not listen to what the prophets are prophesying to you; they fill you with false hopes. They speak visions from their own minds, not from the mouth of the LORD" (Jer. 23:16).

There is a difference between a God-inspired vision and a collection of good ideas. If you have a great idea but it hasn't come as a vision from God, simply relate your idea and let people consider it. But don't categorize it as a vision. A vision from God will ring true and resonate with spiritually sensitive people who will recognize it as inspired of God.

The Value of a Dream

Not much happens without a dream. And for something great to happen there must always be a great dream. Behind every great achievement is a dreamer of great dreams. Much more than a dream is required to bring it to reality; but the dream must be there first.

—Robert Greenleaf

Daniel, the Champion Visionary

The word *vision* appears in the book of Daniel more than any other book of the Bible. God entrusted Daniel with various visions and gave him the ability to interpret the visions of others, notably King Belshazzar (Dan. 5:1ff).

We may never achieve the heights of the vision-receiving and vision-interpreting skills of Daniel, but we certainly can receive a vision from the Lord. Don't be surprised if the vision of what God wants to do in and through you and your church overwhelms you.

Confidence to Speak His Vision

In examining ourselves and in searching for God's direction, we may conclude as Paul did, "Who is equal to such a task?" (2 Cor. 2:16). Yet God never gives a vision that cannot be implemented in his power. Like Paul we may confess that "our competence comes from God. He has made us competent as ministers of a new covenant" (2 Cor. 3:5–6).

As Benjamin Zander, conductor of the Boston Philharmonic Orchestra, said, "Goals can be energizing—when you win. But a vision is more powerful than a goal. A vision is enlivening, it's spirit-giving, it's the guiding force behind all great human endeavors. Vision is about shared energy, a sense of awe, a sense of possibility."[7]

If that is true about a human vision, a great inspiring plan that motivates human endeavor, think of the possibilities if your vision is from God and is destined to make a difference for his kingdom.

A Distinctive Vision

Many pastors begin their ministry in small churches in which they are the only paid staff. A pastor's staff at that point will be all volunteer. Whether leading volunteers or paid staff, the senior pastor needs to be sure he or she understands the difference between a

Tips for Engaging Volunteers in the Church's Vision

1. Reach spiritual leaders through modeling.
2. Engage spiritual leaders through mentoring.
3. Develop spiritual leaders through maturing.

vision and the church's mission. How does a vision differ from the church's purpose or philosophy of ministry?

Aubrey Malphurs, senior professor of pastoral ministries at Dallas Theological Seminary, wrote a helpful article in which he distinguished between three terms that have often been used synonymously with vision: purpose, mission, and philosophy of ministry.[8]

Purpose

A purpose statement for a church answers the question, "Why does the church exist?" Vision, on the other hand, answers the question, "What is the church supposed to accomplish in its community and in its world-wide outreach?"

The purpose statements of many churches will sound similar because they are theologically based. For instance, a church might use Romans 15:6 to help define its purpose: "So that with one heart and mouth you may glorify the God and Father of our Lord Jesus Christ."

Mission

The mission of most churches will also be similar because Jesus gave us the mission in the Great Commission: "Therefore go and make disciples of all nations, baptizing them in the name of the Father and of the Son and of the Holy Spirit, and teaching them to obey everything I have commanded you. And surely I am with you always, to the very end of the age" (Matt. 28:19–20).

Both mission and vision answer the "What?" question in that they speak to what the church's ministry should be. However, the mission of the church is rooted in the biblical command of Christ to "go and make disciples." If a church is not doing this, it is appropriate to question whether it is fulfilling a biblical mission.

Philosophy of Ministry

A philosophy of ministry is based on the church's core values. What are the basic things a church values as it moves forward to engage in ministry? The number of core values will vary from church to church, but usually consists of three to seven biblical values. This might include such things as a commitment to prayer, excellence, growth, lay ministry, and so forth. But each church's philosophy of ministry, while biblical and realistic, will be unique. It may take into consideration the church's unique location or capabilities.

Vision

Vision paints a picture. Vision helps people see what ministry will look like as it is done in and through this particular church in this particular setting. A clear vision will help people know what a church's ministry will look like in two, five, or ten years. Vision takes the mission statement and fleshes it out in terms of what it will look like in this particular community. The more vividly the pastor can paint the picture, the easier it will be for people to see and understand the vision.

Vision Is Not Consensus

We are more likely to express a captivating vision *from* God if we have first had a motivating vision *of* God. Isaiah told us about his vision and how it motivated him to accept God's mission to go and tell others. Before he was motivated to go, he was captivated by a fresh vision of God. He "saw the Lord seated on a throne, high and exalted, and the train of his robe filled the temple" (Isa. 6:1).

So the pastor does not receive a vision by consulting with his or her staff. It is not a matter of consensus; they may provide input; they will certainly have opinions about the direction of the church. But the pastor, before sharing with the staff, will need to spend time with the Lord.

Comparing Purpose, Vision, Mission, and Philosophy of Ministry[9]

Type of Statement	What It Answers	Its Orientation
Purpose	Why does the church exist?	**Theologically** oriented—What is the church's reason for being?
Vision	What is the church supposed to accomplish in ministry?	**Seeing** oriented—What do we see in our heads as the vision is cast for us?
Mission	What is the church's ministry?	**Objective** oriented—What does our plan look like?
Philosophy of Ministry	Why do we do what we do?	**Value** oriented—What shapes our congregational culture?

Let God Expand Your Vision

As you spend time alone with God to seek his vision for your church, you may find that his ideas are greater than yours. Don't be surprised. Remember, the Lord said, "As the heavens are higher than the earth, so are my ways higher than your ways and my thoughts than your thoughts" (Isa. 55:9).

A great vision will honor God and attract people. Henrietta Mears, considered the most innovative Christian educator of her day, said, "There is no magic in small plans. When I consider my ministry, I think of the world. Anything less than that would not be worthy of Christ nor His will for my life."[10]

Let Faith Bolster Your Vision

A God-honoring, need-meeting vision will stretch your faith. Remember how God challenged Abraham to count the stars in the sky and count the sand on the seashore? To the old patriarch, it must have been mind-boggling to think that God was going to make of him a great nation. But "against all hope, Abraham in hope believed, and so became the father of many nations, . . . being fully persuaded that God had power to do what he had promised" (Rom. 4:18, 21).

Hudson Taylor, the great missionary to China, said, "We have heard of many people who trust God too little, but have you ever heard of anyone who trusted Him too much?"[11] Don't worry that your faith will have you running ahead of God. You can't run that fast!

Vision Affects Priorities

When you declare your vision, it becomes a matter of record. Your vision affects the goals you want to reach, the records you want to break, the finish lines you want to cross. A challenging goal tends to motivate us. First, we make the goal; then the goal makes us as it pulls us toward it.

If your vision paints a picture of more people attending your church, more young people involved in the youth ministry, and more boys and girls actively participating in the children's ministry, you and your staff can no longer sit idly on the sidelines. Your vision implies that you and your staff will work toward making the vision a reality. Thus, your priorities for the next six months or a year will incorporate steps toward actualizing your dream.

Staff Alignment with Vision

The pastor who wants to lead his or her staff in discovering the attainable dream will need to take leadership responsibility seriously. It doesn't happen by accident. Dreams and visions from the Lord seldom leap at us unexpectedly. It may come easier to some, those who are by nature more visionary personalities. But all of us can become more visionary by spending time with God and asking him to direct us in the way we should go. The last time I checked, the proverb was still there: "Trust in the LORD with all your heart; do not depend on your own understanding. Seek his will in all you do, and he will show you which path to take" (Prov. 3:5–6 NLT).

Articulate the Vision

David Rockefeller once said, "The number one function of the top executive is to establish the purpose of the organization."[12] For the pastor, this means articulating the vision. Where is this church going? How will we get there? What does our preferred future look like?

We might compare it to spelunking, exploring caves. Imagine you're the leader and the people you are leading have never been in this particular cave. You are the only one who has a flashlight. It's your responsibility to get the people through this experience and back into the sunshine.

Without your light, the people may well become so frightened they turn around and exit the cave without finding all the delights the cave holds. As the leader, it is your responsibility to shine the light, give them confidence, and show them where to go. A vision is like a light in a dark place. You must shine it. You must articulate the vision so the people become enlightened about the direction you are heading.[13]

Communicate Frequently

You must communicate your vision often. People tend to drift off course if they are not reminded periodically of the direction chosen. Remember that the church is your life. You live and breathe it, and it constantly occupies your attention. That is not true of your laypeople. It will probably not be true of your staff, at least not to the same degree it is true of you. So you must articulate the vision often. You are to "say it simply, boldly, repeat it often."[14]

Dialogue with Your Staff Members

Once you have articulated the vision, you will need to sit down with your staff members and talk about how it affects their ministries. How does the overall vision for the church impact the youth, children's, women's, and men's ministries? What changes need to occur to make each ministry align with the direction the church is taking? What new goals need to be set to implement the vision?

Giving Vision to Others

A vision we give to others of who and what they could become has power when it echoes what the Spirit has already spoken into their souls.

—Larry Crabb

Evaluate Your Progress

I know of pastors who will tell you they are evangelistic. They want to win souls. They will declare this as one of their highest priorities. But if you look at their annual report, you do not see this reflected in the number of persons who have received Christ into their lives. I wonder how long it has been since they seriously evaluated their church's ministry. I wonder if they have ever aligned their practice with their declared vision.

You may not feel that administration is your primary spiritual gift. Then you need to bring someone alongside you who has that gift to help analyze where you are compared with where you want to be.

Don't Settle for Mediocrity

The nature of life dictates that things drift. Without a motor, a boat would drift downstream. Without a steady hand on the wheel of the ship, it drifts off course. Without consistent, steady leadership, a church drifts away from its intended goals.

Chuck Swindoll observed, "Without the motivation of divinely empowered insight and enthusiasm, people tend toward the 'average,' doing just enough to get by. Thus, the fallout from the system is mediocrity. . . . Excellence is not only lost in the shuffle, whenever it rears its head, it is considered a threat."[15]

Attaining the Dream

Without dampening the enthusiasm of the new youth minister, the senior pastor in our opening story expanded the vision of Pastor Tim. Just asking the question about what percentage of the high school students were part of the church's youth group painted a picture of an attainable dream for the young man. He was sharp enough to catch the vision right away and went on to build a large and solid youth ministry.

A senior pastor not only has to impart vision to the board and the members of the congregation, but with staff persons to be sure they are on board too. Any serious differences between the lead pastor's vision and the staff pastor's dreams can lead to serious consequences.

By using a little creativity and building on solid relationships with staff, the senior pastor can assist staff persons in discovering an attainable dream for their ministries in the church. Working closely together can ensure that the dreams align so the church moves in one direction.

Action Steps

1. Plan a time to dialogue with staff members about your vision for the church.
2. Evaluate the relationships you have with your staff members. Are there areas of tension? How will you resolve those tensions in order to ensure you are all working on common goals?
3. Check your vision's focus. Is it unclear in any way or is it specific? How can you refine it to improve its focus?

4

Strategy
Creating the Ministry Pathway

Moving your church forward requires a strategy; leading your staff in strategic planning is part of your strategy.

You gotta be careful if you don't know where you're going, otherwise you might not get there.
—Yogi Berra

A woman took her mother to see a field of daffodils. The breathtaking sight included flowers that were a variety of colors—deep orange, white, lemon yellow, salmon pink, saffron, and butter yellow.

When her mother asked who had planted all those daffodils, the daughter answered, "Just one woman." They walked up to a house by the field and on the patio was a poster that said, "Answers to the Questions I Know You Are Asking."

Answer number one: 50,000 bulbs.

Answer number two: one at a time, by one woman. Two hands, two feet, and very little brain.

Answer number three: began in 1958.

The woman pondered: "What might I have accomplished if I had thought of a wonderful goal thirty-five or forty years ago and had worked away at it 'one bulb at a time' through all those years. Just think what I might have been able to achieve!"

The difference between a dream and an accomplishment is a strategy. The daffodil planter had a strategy. And so must we if we expect to take our God-given vision and turn it into reality.

Creative Strategy

Dr. Charles Stanley devised a strategy to help his daughter bail out on her wedding day if she had decided that's what she wanted to do.

Just before he walked her down the aisle, he said, "Becky, if you are standing at the altar and change your mind about this whole thing, just wink. I'll pass out on the floor and bring the entire ceremony to a halt!"[1]

That's a creative strategy, to be sure.

In leading your staff to implement your God-given vision, keep in mind what a strategy is. Strategy is the plan for accomplishing the vision. It incorporates all relevant considerations in a way that provides the most effective means of getting the job done.

Across the years, I have encountered pastors who could cast a vision, but the vision never became a reality. They seemed quite capable of dreaming a great dream, but getting it off the page and into the life of the church was another matter.

Is Planning Unspiritual?

Some pastors seem to have the idea that planning is unspiritual. They think that people who simply trust the Lord will accomplish things in a way that is more spiritual. But this is a misinterpretation of Scriptures that tell us to seek the will of God. "Planning is no more than an attempt to understand the will of God for [your] church and respond to it by our actions."[2]

Far from being unspiritual, planning is a recognition that God wants us to do our best and plan to accomplish our best for him. Brother Andrew said, "At the spiritual level, planning means taking the initiative. It's not about sitting around until you are absolutely certain God is calling you to a particular task, direction, country, or ministry. Nor is it waiting for the doors to open so you can go there easily. Planning is an act of faith. Jesus never told his disciples to wait for an invitation. He told them to go."[3]

Planning Foiled by Fear

Unfortunately a great dream may languish because of fear. Perhaps it is fear of failure. We hesitate to make specific plans because we don't want to lose face if we can't accomplish everything we set out to do. Henry David Thoreau was a great believer in the power of the individual to achieve. He said, "I know of no more encouraging fact than the unquestionable ability of man to elevate his life by conscious endeavor."[4]

If we have that much ability and potential on our own, think how much more competent we can be when we work in the power of the Holy Spirit. Going into partnership with God is one of the greatest enterprises known to the human race. Paul said, "I planted the seed, Apollos watered it, but God made it grow. So neither he who plants nor he who waters is anything, but only God, who makes things grow" (1 Cor. 3:6–7).

Excuses for Not Planning

Others may use the excuse, "I have no money. To accomplish the things we need to do, we need great financial resources, and it's just not there. Have you looked at the economy lately?"

Business philosopher Jim Rohn used that excuse for a while. He told his mentor, "If I had more money, I would have a better plan." His mentor quickly responded, "I would suggest that if you had a better plan, you would have more money." In relating that incident, Rohn added, "You see, it's not the amount that counts; it's the plan that counts."[5]

Dream First

There are those who work all day, those who dream all day, and those who spend an hour dreaming before setting to work to fulfill those dreams. Go into the third category because there's virtually no competition.

—Steven J. Ross

When we work on our strategy, we'll discover that money is not the problem. Money tends to flow toward great ideas. If you work on your strategy, resources will come. So, let's put the excuses behind us.

Proverbs on Planning

I mentioned earlier that some people think it is unspiritual or unbiblical to plan. But just the opposite is true. A person who thinks it is unbiblical to plan obviously is not familiar with the message of the Bible. As someone pointed out, "It pays to plan ahead. It wasn't raining when Noah built the ark."

The book of Proverbs is full of statements about planning. The wise man wrote down so many pithy ideas on this topic (what we might call strategizing), that it is truly impressive. For instance, in Proverbs 15:22, he said, "Plans fail for lack of counsel, but with many advisers they succeed." This simply reminds us that we don't have to generate all the great ideas ourselves. The people we gather around us may supply many more (and better) ideas if we can encourage them to brainstorm with us.

Don't Boast about Lack of Planning

The wise man said, "Wise people think before they act; fools don't—and even brag about their foolishness!" (Prov. 13:16 NLT). It truly is foolish to boast about a lack of planning. One professor of homiletics said that some student preachers refused to study before preaching. They quoted the passage that says, "Do not worry about what to say or how to say it. At that time you will be given what to say, for it will not be you speaking, but the Spirit of your Father speaking through you" (Matt. 10:19–20). They conveniently left off the first part of the verse that begins, "But when they arrest you." It does not say, "When you stand up to preach." So, said the professor, those expecting the Holy Spirit to fill their mouths when they stepped into the pulpit may discover he filled it with hot air!

Similarly, we should not expect God to bless our lack of planning. Indeed, as the ancient writer said, "Wise people think before they act." The wise man went on to say, "A simple man believes anything, but a prudent man gives thought to his steps" (Prov. 14:15).

So on the one hand, we should not make light of planning. On the other hand, we should talk to the Lord, seek his will, and ask for his wisdom in moving ahead. Here again, the wise man offered sage advice: "Commit to the LORD whatever you do, and your plans will succeed" (Prov. 16:3).

The Bible Is Not Anti-Planning

Perhaps verses like the following have caused some people to think it is foolish to plan: "In his heart a man plans his course, but the LORD determines his steps" (Prov. 16:9). The writer did not intend to discourage planning with this verse. Rather, he knew that our best strategies may fail if we do not have the Lord's blessing.

After all, the Lord is watching over us and knows how to guide our steps in the best possible ways.

Another verse that some may have misinterpreted is this: "Many are the plans in a man's heart, but it is the Lord's purpose that prevails" (Prov. 19:21). Indeed, human beings are capable of conjuring up all kinds of ideas, strategies, and plans. But this verse is intended as a caution against planning apart from the Lord. We know he wants to direct our future. In a previous chapter, I cited the wise man's counsel: "Seek his will in all you do, and he will show you which path to take" (Prov. 3:6 NLT).

Good planning and sound strategy will go a long way toward enabling us to bring our God-given vision to realization. The wise man would agree. He said, "The plans of the diligent lead to profit as surely as haste leads to poverty" (Prov. 21:5).

So the Bible commends diligence and cautions against haste. The Bible extols trusting in the Lord and warns against depending only on our own thinking. The Bible acclaims trusting in the Lord's purpose and admonishes against relying solely on our own plans. It speaks well of wise people who think before they act and advises against foolish people who boast about their lack of planning. And finally, the Bible congratulates those who seek wise counsel and rebukes those who proceed without asking for help.

Nehemiah, the Ultimate Planner

Nehemiah was the ultimate planner. When he became aware that the wall in Jerusalem lay in disrepair, he grieved, but then, we can assume, he quickly began to strategize. He thought through what needed to be done so that when the king asked him why his countenance was downcast, he was ready with his plans.

He convinced the king to allow him to leave his post and travel back to Jerusalem in order to rebuild the wall around the city. Nehemiah influenced the king to give financial support to the building program he envisioned. Further, he was able to secure letters from the king to the governors of the surrounding areas, asking them to provide safe conduct as Nehemiah traveled to Jerusalem.

He procured a letter from the king to Asaph, keeper of the king's forest, to provide adequate lumber for rebuilding the city gates. He also obtained a letter from the king naming Nehemiah governor of Judah. Once he arrived in Jerusalem, he organized and equipped the people to do the work. He rallied the people behind him and they accomplished the rebuilding of the wall in record time.

It all began with a vision of what could be done and a clear strategy as to how he could accomplish it—with God's help, the king's help, and the help of the people in Jerusalem.

Turning the Theoretical into the Practical

As I said earlier in this chapter, strategy is what takes a vision and turns it into reality. A strategy fills the gap between dreaming it and doing it. A strategy takes the theoretical and turns it into the practical—but not unless there is the will to move forward toward some concrete goal.

Strategy Requires an Effort of the Will

Basketball coach Bobby Knight said, "The will to succeed is important, but what's more important is the will to prepare."[6] His statement makes perfect sense on the basketball court. What happens in a game is a direct result of practice and preparation.

But the same is true in pursuing a goal. Unless one takes the vision and reduces it to strategic steps, it always remains in the realm of the theoretical. Nothing is sadder than a dream that has died for lack of a plan, a strategy, or some practical steps toward accomplishment.

Strategy Brings Dreams to Realization

A clear relationship exists between vision and strategy, between your dream and your plans. A clear strategy is the key. Thinking it through. Writing it down. Breaking it down into bite-sized pieces. These are all ways of pulling your vision out of the intangible and giving it flesh, forcing it to become a reality.

Strategy Involves Overcoming Obstacles

Of course, forming a strategy does not guarantee immunity from obstacles. You may come from poor circumstances. You may encounter opposition. You may face innumerable obstacles. These may be the cards life has dealt you. Yet developing a clear strategy often includes how to get over, under, around, or through the things that prevent your vision from becoming a reality.

Your mission is to overcome the Enemy who wants to drag as many souls to hell as possible. And your goal is to expand the kingdom of God and reach as many for Christ as possible.

Strategy Attracts Resources

It is amazing how resources will flow once you work your strategy toward achieving your goals. It is almost as if people, money, and resources of all kinds are just waiting on the sidelines. When you announce your dream and begin to move toward it, these resources begin to flow toward your great idea.

Strategy Requires Commitment

There is no substitute for commitment. A strong commitment to pursuing your vision with a well-thought strategy will provide impetus toward the results you want.

William Booth, founder (along with his wife Catherine) of the Salvation Army, was diagnosed with blindness when he was in his eighties. His doctor left it to Bramwell, Booth's son, to tell him the news.

"You mean that I am going blind?"

"Well, General, I fear that we must contemplate that." (The family always addressed their father affectionately as "General.")

The father then asked his son, "I shall never see your face again?"

"No, probably not in this world."

Booth was quiet for a few moments. Then he took his son's hand and said, "God must know best!" Another pause, then, "Bramwell, I have done what I could for God and for the people with my eyes. Now I shall do what I can for God and for the people without my eyes."[7]

No wonder the Salvation Army was so successful. And your enterprise will be successful too when you pursue your strategy with firm commitment, and with the help of God.

Teaching Strategic Planning

Teaching your staff to plan strategically is one of the most important things you can do. Most of us graduate from Bible college or seminary and we are ready to do ministry. We can't wait to get in the trenches, work with people, and find out what ministry is all about. We all need those kinds of hands-on experiences. We all need the practical experience of doing ministry firsthand.

Sometimes we are so busy doing ministry that we don't take time to engage in strategic planning. But as Jim Rohn pointed out, "Success is 20 percent skills and 80 percent strategy. You might know how to read, but more importantly, what's your plan to read?"[8] Rohn was trying to motivate people to read more, but his statement is true for whatever you are doing. One of the best things you can teach your staff is the importance of doing strategic planning.

Dream First

Aim at heaven and you will get earth thrown in. Aim at earth and you get neither.

—C. S. Lewis

Here are a few of the things involved in helping staff learn how to get from here to there, how to reach the target, whatever that might be.

Take Inventory of Your Resources

What kinds of facilities will you need if you achieve your goals? What do you have now? What financial resources do you have, compared to what you will need? And most important, what kind of human resources do you have? Who are the people most likely to line up to help? Whom do you need to recruit to come alongside and help?

A colleague has told about a youth pastor whose program was so successful that he outgrew the facilities. There was no longer any room in the church large enough to accommodate the group, except the sanctuary, which was not conducive to the type of program he envisioned. Some strategic planning involved researching not only the rooms available on the premises, but also looking at what buildings were available in the immediate area. The building just two doors away from the church held possibilities. Strategizing enabled the youth pastor to develop a plan to purchase the building and renovate it into a youth center.

What Can You Delegate?

Staff persons who are used to doing it all themselves will need to learn that they accomplish more by delegating than by doing the job all by themselves.

A new minister of visitation did a great job of following up on visitors. He connected successfully with many of them and succeeded in incorporating them into the life of the church. But his success multiplied when he learned to train others to do the visitation. It was the difference between doing ministry and equipping people to do ministry. A strategy session between the minister of visitation and the senior pastor opened the door to the possibilities. Further strategy sessions outlined a plan to recruit and train the volunteers.

Developing Lay Leaders

There are several reasons why it is profitable to develop lay leaders:

1. Lay leadership honors Christ.
2. It fulfills spiritual giftedness.
3. It ministers to others.

Set Long-, Medium-, and Short-Range Goals to Achieve the Vision

All of us need goals to help us stay on course. Without goals, we are like the boy who shot arrows into the side of the barn and then drew bull's-eyes around them. With a strategy like that, you win every time, but it's winning by default, not by true strategic planning. We have all heard the old saying, "When you fail to plan, you plan to fail." Clear goals keep us from going down the road to failure.

Goal-setting will be discussed further in the next chapter, but for now suffice it to say that if your staff members are not experienced in goal-setting, one of your important assignments is to show them how to do it and hold them accountable for the goals they set.

Big Goals/No Goals

Big goals get big results.
No goals get no results or somebody else's results.

—Mark Victor Hansen

Have You Lined Up the Right People Doing the Right Things?

When Jim Collins wrote his best-selling book *Good to Great*, he said one of the most important factors executives of "Good to Great" companies discovered was to get the right people on the bus. The executives said, in essence, "Look, I don't really know where we should take this bus. But I know this much: If we get the right people on the bus, the right people in the right seats, and the wrong people off the bus, then we'll figure out how to take it someplace great."[9]

We have all known people who were wired in such a way that it didn't matter what they did, they would succeed. Whatever they touched turned to gold, or at least improved significantly. As you and your staff members look around, you will find the best people available to you.

"But, Stan," I hear you say, "what if we look around and don't find the caliber of people you're talking about? I have looked around and I'm not impressed!" First, be sure you are looking at people through the right set of lenses. If you are wearing cynical, critical, or jaded lenses, it will affect your judgment. Second, if you don't find the caliber of people you want, go find some. There are people in your community who can help you. You just have to find them. Third, engage in leadership development. Some of the people you may have written off are indeed capable, but they need guidance, training, encouragement, and the investment of your leadership.

Help your staff see these principles and either find the right people, recruit them, or develop them. Be sure you get the right people on the bus. As Collins says, "Great vision without great people is irrelevant."[10]

How Will You Measure Progress?

I will have more to say about measuring the progress of your goals in the next chapter, but for now, understand that if you can't measure it, you probably need to reword it, make it more specific, give it a definite deadline. After all, a goal is simply a dream with a deadline. Part of the strategy you want to communicate to your staff is the importance of putting reasonable deadlines on your goals.

Getting Started

Wherever you need to go, the first step is to begin. A day at the beach is not swimming if you never stick your toe in the water. It's just sunbathing. To swim, you have to test the water, stick in your toe, and wade up to your ankles, your knees, your waist, and then plunge into the water and swim.

Whether you're planting daffodils or building a great church, you need a plan. You and your staff will need to develop a strategy. Chart your course as specifically as possible and get started.

Action Steps

1. When can you schedule a strategic planning session with your staff? Do it.
2. Have you used excuses to keep from planning? Stop now and determine to plan.
3. Take inventory of your resources for action: human, financial, and facilities.

5

Goals
Setting Useful Milestones

Both you and your staff must set worthwhile personal goals.

If you go to work on your goals, your goals will go to work on you.
—Jim Rohn

According to an old fable, once upon a time a Sea Horse gathered his pieces of eight (the Spanish dollar, a silver coin) and decided to swim out to seek his fortune. He hadn't traveled far when he met an Eel, who said, "Psst! Hey, Bud, where ya goin'?"

"I'm going out to seek my fortune."

"You're in luck," said the Eel. "For four pieces of eight you can have this speedy flipper and then you'll be able to get there a lot faster."

"That's great!" said the Sea Horse. He paid the money and raced off at twice the speed. Soon he encountered a Sponge, who said, "Psst! Hey, Bud, where ya goin'?"

"I'm going out to seek my fortune."

"You're in luck," said the Sponge. "For a few pieces of eight I will let you have this jet-propelled scooter and then you'll be able to get there a lot faster."

So the Sea Horse bought the scooter with his remaining money and zoomed off at five times the speed. Soon he encountered a Shark, who said, "Psst! Hey, Bud, where ya goin'?"

"I'm going out to seek my fortune."

"You're in luck. If you will take this shortcut," said the Shark, pointing to his mouth, "you'll save yourself a lot of time."

"Thanks!" said the Sea Horse, and zipped off into the interior of the Shark—there to be devoured!

The moral to this quaint fable is that if you don't know where you're going and how you're going to get there, you may just wind up someplace else and not even know it.[1]

People who go through life without goals, depending on chance to get where they want to go, are likely to be disappointed. The same God who planned the universe with such intricate detail has given us brains to set reasonable, but ambitious, goals that will maximize our potential and bring glory to him.

Why People Don't Set Goals

Life without goals is like a football game without an end zone. Or a basketball game without a backboard, hoop, and basket. People soon lose interest if there is no goal in sight.

Zig Ziglar, who has been called America's motivational speaker, lists four reasons why people do not have a goal-setting program.[2]

Fear

Fear inhibits people from succeeding in life. Whether it's fear of the unknown, failure, or some other paralyzing phobia, fear has led many people to stop before they gave it their best effort.

You wouldn't think of embarking on a cross-country trip without consulting a map or at least programming your GPS to help you get there. Yet many people go through life with no clear sense of direction as to where they want to go and how they're going to get there.

Poor Self-Image

One of the main problems with poor self-esteem is that people who have a negative self-image tend to see themselves in the worst possible light. They also tend to gravitate toward others who are negative, further reinforcing their low opinion of themselves. If we are already convinced that we won't amount to much, we have no motivation to achieve anything for the future.

Low self-esteem keeps us from setting goals or even caring about goals. If we feel inferior, we may believe that others can achieve great things, but we can't seem to see ourselves in the same light.

Not Understanding the Benefits of Setting Goals

The benefits of setting goals are enormous. David G. Jensen, chief administrative officer for the Crump Institute of Biological Imaging for the UCLA School of Medicine, surveyed people who attended Zig Ziglar's seminars. He organized them into two groups: those who set goals and those who took no specific action to set goals.

He discovered the goal setters earned an average of $7,401 each month, while the non-action group earned $3,397 a month. Financial benefits are not the only ones to consider, but we look at them first because they're easy to count. In addition to the financial benefits, Jensen found that the action group tended to be more enthusiastic, more satisfied with life and work, happier in marriage, and had overall better health.

Jensen added, "These results also confirm the academic literature on goals that, over the past 20 years, has shown unequivocally that those who set goals perform better in a variety of tasks."[3]

So what are the reasons we should set goals? Who will benefit if we set goals?

Personal Reasons. What motivates you? What meaningful goal gives you a warm inner glow? Is there an inner satisfaction that you have done the will of God? Is there a sense in which you feel you have done something of significance?

I have heard of millionaires who continue to work ten to twelve hours a day, making more money. It isn't the money; it's the journey. They keep at it because of the joy they experience in accomplishing something worthwhile.

I have heard people say, "If I had a million dollars, I'd never work another day in my life." Business philosopher Jim Rohn observes, "That's probably why the good Lord sees to it that he doesn't get his million. Because he would just quit."[4]

Family. Sometimes we will do things for other people that we wouldn't do for ourselves. But think of spending quality time with each of your children, your spouse, or other family members or friends. What long-range, mid-range, and short-range goals do you have for your family?

I heard about a pastor's wife who said her husband is so busy that he often misses the evening meal. When he showed up for dinner one evening, one of his children said, "Dad, what are you doing here eating with us?" That's a pretty good clue that it's time to set some goals that will benefit the family.

God, the Church, and His Kingdom. Some of the goals you set will affect the future of your church. When you realize that the goals you set may directly affect who may or may not be reached with the gospel, it adds a note of seriousness to goal-setting. And we should be serious. Not grim, but serious.

Don't Know How to Develop a Goal-Setting Plan

If you have never thought seriously about goal-setting, you may not even know how to go about it. At best, your ideas about goal-setting may be fuzzy. Fuzzy thinking and fuzzy planning get fuzzy results.

Later in this chapter, I will talk about some practical steps in developing a goal-setting plan. In the meantime, what does the Bible say about goal-setting? Is this a biblical concept or is it only a humanistic mechanism to get more out of life?

Whatever You Vividly Imagine

Paul J. Meyer said, "Whatever you vividly imagine, ardently desire, sincerely believe, and enthusiastically act upon must inevitably come to pass."[5] Is that simply a catchy, success-oriented, self-help mantra; or has Meyer, knowingly or unknowingly, captured an idea that has a basis in biblical teaching?

Vividly Imagine

It is not difficult to find biblical characters who vividly imagined the future. Isaiah, Ezekiel, Daniel, and the apostle John wrote about a future that boggles the imagination. When Stuart Briscoe wrote his book on Ezekiel, he titled it, *All Things Weird and Wonderful*.

Paul wrote, "No eye has seen, no ear has heard, no mind has conceived what God has prepared for those who love him—but God has revealed it to us by his Spirit" (1 Cor. 2:9–10). So whatever your dreams and plans for the future, you are not likely to think bigger than God is thinking!

Dream Your Dream

Hudson Taylor was converted at the age of seventeen after reading a tract from his father's library. Early on, he had a dream to serve others in China, where he did serve for fifty-one years, founding a new mission society, the China Inland Mission. By the time of his death in 1905, he had established twenty mission stations, brought 849 missionaries to the field, and trained an additional 700 Chinese workers. Some estimate he baptized 50,000 Chinese people, as many as 35,000 of them being people he had personally led to Christ.

Ardently Desire

Meyer also said we should "ardently desire." The psalmist agreed when he said, "May he give you the desire of your heart and make all your plans succeed" (Ps. 20:4). When you read that verse in context, you see that the psalmist is not envisioning simply a humanistic plan. He envisioned a person who was trusting in God to bring his plans to pass: "Some trust in chariots and some in horses, but we trust in the name of the LORD our God" (Ps. 20:7).

Sincerely Believe

Those who set goals must "sincerely believe" in the object of their goal-setting. If you do not believe in what you are pursuing, why are you pursuing it? Moses planted a goal in the heart of Caleb before the people of Israel ever entered the Promised Land. He said, "The land on which your feet have walked will be your inheritance and that of your children forever, because you have followed the LORD my God wholeheartedly" (Josh. 14:9).

Caleb held on to that promise and believed in it wholeheartedly. When they finally stood in Canaan, having crossed the Jordan River into the Promised Land, he said to Joshua, "Now then, just as the LORD promised, he has kept me alive for forty-five years since the time he said this to Moses, while Israel moved about in the desert. So here I am today, eighty-five years old! I am still as strong today as the day Moses sent me out; I'm just as vigorous to go out to battle now as I was then. Now give me this hill country that the LORD promised me that day. You yourself heard then that the Anakites were there and their cities were large and fortified, but, the LORD helping me, I will drive them out just as he said" (Josh. 14:10–12).

Enthusiastically Act

It's difficult to imagine anyone who would "enthusiastically act upon" the goal he envisioned more than Caleb did! From our introduction to him in the book of Numbers, we discover he was a person who saw the glass half full instead of half empty. While the majority of the spies who entered Canaan to explore its cities, inhabitants, and resources were negative and overwhelmed with the impossibilities, Caleb was positive. While the majority had their eyes on the large, well-fortified cities, and the gigantic inhabitants, Caleb had his eye on God's power.

After hearing the negative report, "Caleb silenced the people before Moses and said, 'We should go up and take possession of the land, for we can certainly do it'" (Num. 13:30). Although the majority saw themselves as grasshoppers compared to the inhabitants of Canaan, Caleb insisted to "not be afraid of the people of the land, because we will swallow them up. Their protection is gone, but the LORD is with us. Do not be afraid of them" (Num. 14:9).

When he said, "We will swallow them up," it was like saying, "We can defeat them as easily as we can swallow a piece of bread." In other words, "It's a piece of cake!" And when he said, "Their protection is gone," perhaps he was thinking of the protection the Lord constantly provided the people of Israel with the pillar of cloud by day and the pillar of fire by night. While the Israelites had God's covering, the inhabitants of Canaan had no such protection.

Caleb personifies the spirit of those who "vividly imagine, ardently desire, sincerely believe, and enthusiastically act upon" the goals they believe God has set before them.

Underlying Factors in Goal-Setting

Several years ago, a magazine ad pictured a man standing in his office, looking out the window. The caption read: "Why would a company pay this man $100,000 a year to look out the window?"[6] But the fact is, every organization needs someone who is looking out the window toward the future. You may not think of yourself as a visionary, but you need to have a vision. We all need to be persons who set goals and follow through in achieving them.

What Goal-Setting Is Not

Goal-setting is not daydreaming. It is not engaging in fantasy or a substitute for reality. Henry David Thoreau said, "If you have built castles in the air, your work need not be lost; that is where they should be. Now put the foundations under them."[7]

The problem is when we build air castles but never get around to putting foundations under them. This is why one of the best definitions of "goal" is "a dream with a deadline."[8]

The First Step to Positive Action

Before you act, you need to have a direction in which to move. People who have no goals are like those who saddle up and ride off in all directions. It's like shooting an arrow with no target toward which to aim.

A goal is necessary before you take positive action because you need a clear direction to pursue. Otherwise it's like a river with no banks; it simply runs wherever gravity will take it. A cross-country runner needs a course to follow. A race car driver needs a track on which to drive. And you need the direction that a clearly defined, written goal will provide.

Bringing the Future into Focus

As I said earlier, fuzzy thinking brings fuzzy results. Clear goals bring the future into focus. Stephen Strang said, "Setting a goal is like focusing sunlight with a magnifying glass. When your life energy is shining on a pinpoint, you can start a fire."[9]

If that is true—and it is—then we need to be as specific as we can about what we want to accomplish. The person who lacks clear goals often faces the future with apprehension because he or she has no idea of what to expect. But those with clear goals are working toward a specific future with a definite idea of what to expect.

The Magnet Principle

The magnet principle says "like attracts like." You'll attract to you the people, circumstances, events, money and resources you need to accomplish your goals.

—Mark Victor Hansen

Goals have a magnetic quality. They tend to pull you in their direction. The more specific and better defined they are, the more likely they are to pull you in the direction you want to go. Even when difficulties come, you can look through the fog to a clear destination on the other side.

Personal Goals

If I were to hand you a set of goals and say, "Here! Reach these goals!" you might receive them, you might reject them, or you might even resent them. At best, they would be my goals for you, not your own goals for yourself. They would not begin to have the motivating power that forming your own personal goals would have.

A word of warning: Be careful to whom you show your goals. If you know that others will see your personal goals, you will write them with that fact in mind. It will cause you to be less than candid because you will be thinking unconsciously about the image of yourself that you want others to see.

Further, in everybody's life there are firefighters and fire lighters. In our communities, we value firefighters because they keep us safe and protect our property. But in the world of goal-setting, firefighters are those who throw cold water on your great ideas. They douse your enthusiasm and dispel your energy. Fire lighters, on the other hand, are people who fan the flame of your enthusiasm and add to your energy.

Positive Goals

Our minds function through mental images, and it is difficult to visualize a negative. When we express our goals negatively, the mind has trouble visualizing a void or a vacuum. If a person says, "I'm overweight. I'm going to lose twenty pounds," it is difficult to visualize a loss of twenty pounds. However, if a person says,

"I'm going to lose weight until I weigh 170 pounds," that is a mental picture the mind can visualize.

In the 1981 National Football Conference championship game, the Dallas Cowboys led the San Francisco 49ers with two minutes to play. But on the final play, Dwight Clark, not realizing that Joe Montana was trying to throw the ball out of the end zone, jumped up, made the catch, and won the game for San Francisco.

The next day a reporter asked Cowboys president Tex Schramm what happened. He answered that the Cowboys went out there determined not to lose the game. The 49ers went out there determined to win the game. One team's picture was winning; the other's was not losing.[10] Big difference.

Realistic, Attainable Goals

Realistic and attainable does not mean your goals must be low, mediocre, or commonplace. Instead, they must be goals toward which you are able and willing to work. Your goals should represent significant progress. You will not be motivated if your goals do not demand worthwhile effort to reach them.

A high goal is often easier to reach than a low goal, because a high goal has greater motivational power. You know it's going to take more effort, but you also know it will be worth the effort. You will never reach a substantial goal with a halfhearted approach.

Goals That Stretch

Great companies have unattainable goals that propel their organizations to greatness. For example, a small Japanese company not long after WWII set a goal of making the phrase "Made in Japan" synonymous with quality at a time when it meant cheap. The name of that small company: Sony. Another small company set this goal in the late 1970s: "A computer on every desk; a computer in every home." That company: Microsoft.

—Stephen Strang

Written Goals

Some anonymous writer said, "Until you commit your goals to paper you have intentions that are seeds without soil."

Write Everything Down. One of the greatest examples of written goals is found in the story of John Goddard. When he was fifteen years old, he sat down and thought about all the things he wanted to do when he grew up. He wrote down everything that occurred to him. Every adventure, journey, challenge, and pleasure, and then one by one, year by year, he set about accomplishing them.

Some were reasonably easy to attain: become an Eagle Scout; type fifty words a minute; visit a movie studio. Others were more difficult: milk a rattlesnake; sail the South Seas in a schooner; visit every country in the world. The last time I checked, he had accomplished 109 of his 127 goals, and had visited all but thirty countries.

Plan for Success

Paul J. Meyer suggested a five-point program for his "Million Dollar Success Plan."

- Crystallize your thinking. Determine what specific goal you want to achieve.
- Develop a plan for achieving your goal, and a deadline for its attainment. Plan your progress carefully: hour by hour, day by day, month by month.
- Develop a sincere desire for the things you want in life. A burning desire is the greatest motivator of every human action.
- Develop supreme confidence in yourself and your own abilities. Enter every activity without giving mental recognition to the possibility of defeat. Concentrate on your strengths, instead of your weaknesses.
- Develop a dogged determination to follow through on your plan, regardless of obstacles, criticism or circumstances or what other people say, think or do.

Don't Prejudge Your Ability. It's easy to say, "My parents never did that. No one else in my family has ever done that." You might say, "I've never pastored a church of that size before. I've never had those kinds of people in my church before. I can't reach out to the mayor of the town. What would I say?"

As long as you keep learning, growing, and living, there's no reason to prejudge your ability. As the lady who lived on the bayou said when she grew tired of hearing her neighbor complain about how tough life was: "You live on the bayou. You can go anywhere from here!"

Practical Aspects to Goal-Setting

It's one thing to be a person committed to goal-setting yourself; it's quite another to cultivate that culture among your staff. So let's consider some steps toward developing that expectation.

Recruit Leaders with Potential

Among the many factors you will want to consider when hiring new staff members is whether the person in question has obvious strengths. Even an executive as effective as Abraham Lincoln did not always get this right. When selecting generals in the early days of the Civil War, Lincoln tended to choose men without glaring weaknesses. U. S. Grant eventually became the person Lincoln needed to win the war. But, according to management expert Peter Drucker, "Before he chose Grant, [Lincoln] had appointed in succession three or four Generals whose main qualifications were their lack of major weaknesses."[11]

A Team Works toward a Common Goal

A well-defined goal unifies a team of laypersons around a common purpose, guides the team's work together, and lets team members know when their purpose has been accomplished. Uniting laypersons to work toward a common goal is a powerful ministry strategy.

Strong people often have strong weaknesses. But if you hire people who have strong qualities of leadership, they are more likely to be the kinds of persons you need, in spite of their weakness, as long as their weaknesses are not moral in nature.

Reveal Your Own Commitment to Goal-Setting

There is no point in trying to convince others of the benefits of goal-setting if you are not a person who sets goals and follows through on them.

When Jim Rohn was twenty-five years old, his mentor, Earl Shoaff, said, "I suggest, Jim, that you set a goal to become a millionaire." In telling that story, Rohn said:

> I was all intrigued by that. You know, it's got a nice ring to it—millionaire.
>
> Then Mr. Shoaff said, "Here's why . . ."
>
> I thought to myself, "He doesn't need to teach me why. Wouldn't it be great to have a million dollars?"
>
> Shoaff said, "No. Then you'll never acquire it. Instead, set a goal to become a millionaire for what it makes of you to achieve it.
>
> "Do it for the skills you have to learn and the person you have to become. Do it for what you'll end up knowing about the marketplace. What you'll learn about the management of time and working with people.
>
> "Do it for the ability of discovering how to keep your ego in check—for what you have to learn about being benevolent. Being kind as well as being strong. What you have to learn about society and business and government and taxes and becoming an accomplished person to reach the status of millionaire.

"All that you have learned and all that you have to become to reach the status of millionaire is what's valuable. Not the million dollars."[12]

Why would I use the example of becoming a millionaire? It's not because of the money. It's because what you need to become is far more valuable than a million dollars. The qualities God wants to build in you are priceless. So become all you can be for God's glory and the sake of his kingdom. And then reveal that commitment to being a goal-directed person to your staff.

Reflect an Expectation for Goal-Setting

Just as the moon reflects the light of the sun to illuminate our nights, so senior pastors reflect their expectation for goal-setting to the staff. Developing this culture in their thinking and behavior is one of the most important things you can do.

Teach your staff members to develop SMART goals:

S—specific
M—measurable
A—attainable
R—relevant
T—trackable[13]

Specific. As I hinted at earlier, the more specific the better. Lily Tomlin once said, "I always wanted to be somebody, but I should have been more specific."[14]

Measurable. How will your staff members know whether they have achieved their goals if they have no way of measuring them?

They may need to break down goals into incremental parts and achieve one piece at a time.

Attainable. Be sure they are attainable. Nothing will discourage staff more quickly than goals that are too high and expect too much progress too soon. Remember the phrase I used earlier—realistic and attainable. Goals should stretch your staff, not break them.

Relevant. By relevant, I mean do the goals represent something your staff really cares about? If the goals aren't personal and positive, the staff is not likely to bring out their best effort.

Trackable. Finally, the best goals are those you can track. Some of today's world-wide delivery companies pride themselves on having a system that enables you to track your package. You know when it was sent, its approximate current location in the process, and when it will be delivered. Likewise, regular accountability sessions with your staff members will give you and them the opportunity to track their progress.

Review Their Progress

Taking time to sit down with your staff members and review their progress reminds them that you take goal-setting seriously. Be sure your staff members know what they are responsible for, when regular feedback will occur, and to whom they are accountable. Unless you're a pastor at a megachurch, your staff members will most likely report to you.

Regular staff meetings give you the opportunity to discuss goals without making staff members feel that they are being called on the carpet. If the only time you discuss goals is at their annual review or when they make a mistake, they associate their goals only with job performance. How much better if they understand it as a way of life, as a way to be most effective?

Stay Out of the Cage

Far from knowing how to develop a goal-setting plan, many people are trapped in prisons of their own making. Veterans of the Vietnam conflict have told about the Viet Cong tiger cage. Because the Communist guerrillas were constantly on the move through the jungles, they kept their POWs in small portable prisons that could be picked up quickly and moved. That's why they invented the "tiger cage," which consisted of bamboo sticks, formed into a little jail that averaged about five feet long and approximately four feet wide, too small for a tall American to stretch out.[15]

Unfortunately, many allow "tiger cages" to be built around their minds. So instead of developing a goal-setting plan, we languish in our cages, unable to think further than next Sunday's sermon.

As you become adept at goal-setting and performance, and as you cultivate these qualities in your staff, you should see effectiveness improve.

By the time Disney World was built in Orlando, Florida, Walt Disney had died. His widow attended the opening ceremonies and dedication for the theme park. Afterwards, someone said to Mrs. Disney, "It's too bad Walt never saw this."

She answered, "Oh, but he did. That's why it's here."[16]

After you and I are long gone, I hope someone can stand somewhere and truthfully say that significant things happened because you and I passed that way.

Action Steps

1. Take some uninterrupted time to write down the things you would most like to accomplish in the next six months, year, and five years. How will you go about achieving these goals?
2. Write down the things you would most like to see your staff accomplish. How and when will you communicate these ideals to your staff members?
3. Who are the fire lighters in your life? The firefighters? How can you be sure the fire lighters have greater access to you than the firefighters?

6

SUPERVISION
EMPOWERING FOR SUCCESS

Leaders are not truly leading unless someone is following; leading includes proper supervision.

The best executive is the one who has sense enough to pick good men to do what he wants done, and self-restraint enough to keep from meddling with them while they do it.
—THEODORE ROOSEVELT

When Don Baker hired Jim, his first full-time youth pastor fresh out of seminary, the young man showed up, full of enthusiasm, and said, "Hi, Boss! What do you want me to do?"

Although Don knew what Jim should do, he was too busy to tell him at that moment, so he told the young man to go to his office, get down on his knees, and ask God what he was supposed to do.

That wasn't altogether bad advice, but it certainly was a cop-out on Baker's part to avoid this responsibility. So, why are we not surprised when, according to Baker, "God kept telling Jim to do the dumbest things"?[1]

This scenario is replicated in various forms all across the church world as senior pastors, faced with the responsibility of supervising staff, flounder because they don't want to take the time to do what the job requires them to do.

Baker was not the only person ever to fail to take enough time with a new staff member. A colleague told me that his relationship with a new staff member improved significantly when he began to meet him for breakfast once a week. Those meetings over hotcakes often revolved around nothing but chatting about family, hobbies, or the latest books they were reading. The secret of their success was not so much about the content of the meetings—which were seldom about church work—but about the fact that they spent time together.

Why Supervision Falls Short

Leadership in the area of staff supervision often falls short for a variety of reasons, sometimes because a leader has not genuinely understood what he or she should do. James McGregor Burns said: "Many acts heralded or bemoaned as instances of leadership—acts of oratory, manipulation, sheer self-advancement, brute coercion—are not such. Much of what commonly passes as leadership—conspicuous position-taking without followers or follow-through, posturing on various public stages, manipulation without general purpose, authoritarianism—is no more leadership than the behavior of small boys marching in front of a parade, who continue to strut along Main Street after the procession has turned down a side street toward the fairgrounds."[2]

Let's look at a few reasons why some pastors do not make good supervisors.

Insecurity

A senior pastor who hires a staff person for the first time may be unprepared for the possible changes that are bound to come. Especially if that staff person carries ministerial credentials, suddenly someone else begins to answer to the title "Pastor." If a senior pastor is insecure, he or she may see a staff member as a competitor rather than a collaborator.

The Barna Research Group and the Fuller Church Growth Institute learned that 70 percent of pastors said their self-image is lower now than when they entered the ministry. Ninety percent reported they feel inadequate for the tasks before them. Seventy-five percent of pastors said they are intimidated by the lay leaders or staff with which they work.[3]

Lack of Experience

Everyone has to start somewhere, so it stands to reason that pastors, at some point, will have their first experience working with staff. My observation over the years indicates that senior pastors typically perform better as a supervisor if they have previously served in a staff position. All of us, reflecting on our experiences, tend to say, "If I were in charge, I would do it this way." Or, "If I were senior pastor, I wouldn't do it like that."

Blessed is the senior pastor who, remembering early experiences of working as a staff person, can translate that into good supervision when given the opportunity.

If you lack experience working with staff, don't despair. Be a student of good supervision, talk to more experienced pastors, read all you can, and learn all you can. Move ahead with sensitivity, and you will succeed.

Fear of Conflict

Les and Leslie Parrot, who work primarily in the area of marriage, said, "Conflict is the only way to intimacy."[4] That is great advice for people working on their marriages, but it is also great insight for people supervising a staff. While staff intimacy is not the same as marriage intimacy, a certain camaraderie is essential if a staff is to work well together.

If conflict is not handled as it arises, its energy goes elsewhere. "Unaired conflict goes into the parking lot or behind closed doors. It becomes 'malicious compliance' and results in artificial harmony, not deep community."[5]

Resolving Conflict

Elmer Towns lists four foundational principles necessary for resolving conflict:

1. Accurate data needs to be collected to make good decisions.
2. Each member involved in the conflict needs to feel they are being treated fairly.
3. Individuals involved in church conflict must maintain a mutual respect for others.
4. Every effort should be expended to achieve a consensus decision.

Not Paying Attention to Results

I have known of staff persons who chafed under the idea of having to produce, of having to obtain results in their particular area of ministry. They sometimes say things like, "God expects us to be faithful. We have to leave the results in his hands."

God does expect us to be faithful. But faithfulness eventually leads to fruitfulness, and fruitfulness spells results. Results are sometimes hard to measure, and sometimes there are extenuating circumstances. A factory closes, businesses go belly-up, and jobs move out of the area, taking valuable church members and contributors away from the congregation. But those conditions will be the exception rather than the general rule. None of those circumstances catch God by surprise. He still has a way for us to find positive results.

If we don't pay attention when reasonable results are not forthcoming, we perpetuate poor performance. Further, we may leave the impression that results don't matter. But they do.

Avoiding Accountability

Holding people accountable is not fun. If you enjoy it, you may be a little sadistic.

Nevertheless, it needs to be done. There's an interesting thing about accountability: When we know someone is holding us accountable, we perform better. We know someone is going to check our work. It happens with students in school, and it happens with employees on a job.

When there is a goal to be reached and we know someone is going to ask us about it, we strive to reach that goal. When there are certain expectations of performance, we endeavor to meet those expectations. We know we will be held accountable at the end of our lives. It doesn't hurt to get into practice now by setting sensible guidelines and expecting staff members to live by them.

The Master Supervisor

Jesus is the master motivator, the master supervisor, and the master at empowering others. By examining the way he dealt with the disciples, we see the Master at work.[6]

He Called Them

"As Jesus walked beside the Sea of Galilee, he saw Simon and his brother Andrew casting a net into the lake, for they were fishermen. 'Come, follow me,' Jesus said, 'and I will make you fishers of men.' At once they left their nets and followed him" (Mark 1:16–18).

His calling for men to follow him is similar to our recruiting others to join us on a church staff. Whether we find a gifted layperson who can take on a staff position, or we interview and hire candidates from college or seminary, we call them to follow our vision and be part of the leadership team.

He Named Them

When Jesus met Peter, he "looked at him and said, 'You are Simon, son of John. You will be called Cephas' (which, when translated, is Peter)" (John 1:42).

We may not have instant insight into the people who work with us as Jesus did. But we do need to get to know them. The Greek word for Peter means *rock*. Jesus knew Peter had it in him to become a rock. The people we work with have potential too. We need to recognize it and develop it.

He Made Them a Team

"Then Jesus went around teaching from village to village. Calling the Twelve to him, he sent them out two by two and gave them authority over evil spirits" (Mark 6:6–7).

I will have more to say about teams in chapter 9, but for now note that Jesus knew the value of teaching people to work together. Those who were fishermen already understood the importance of partnerships and division of labor as they worked their nets, sailed their boats, and provided for their families. We know the lessons of teamwork, along with love and loyalty toward one another, sank in, for later in life, Peter wrote, "Love one another deeply, from the

Working Together

Pastors not only lead staff, they also lead laypersons. Ben Merold offers four things pastors and laypeople need to work together:

1. Prayer—No decisions will be made until we first hold a prayer meeting.
2. Fellowship—It is a mistake to think that elders and staff can be friends in the decision-making process if they are not friends socially.
3. Compassion—A compassionate leadership is necessary if we are to develop a caring congregation.
4. Vision—Leaders must know where they are and where they are going.

heart" (1 Pet. 1:22). John wrote, "Dear children, let us not love with words or tongue but with actions and in truth" (1 John 3:18).

He Trusted Them

"After this the Lord appointed seventy-two others and sent them two by two ahead of him to every town and place where he was about to go" (Luke 10:1).

The Lord gave them a job to do and trusted them to do it. They followed him, observed him, and then did what he did. He gave them instructions and then let them go and gain real life experience as they ministered to others. We can't be everywhere, so we must train others and then release them for ministry.

He Tested Them

"A furious storm came up on the lake, so that the waves swept over the boat. But Jesus was sleeping. The disciples went and woke him, saying, 'Lord, save us! We're going to drown!' He replied, 'You of little faith, why are you so afraid?' Then he got up and rebuked the winds and the waves, and it was completely calm. The men were amazed and asked, 'What kind of man is this? Even the winds and the waves obey him!'" (Matt. 8:24–27).

Imagine experienced fishermen, such as some of them were, being frightened by a storm. This simply tells us it must have been a terrifying storm. Jesus rebuked the storm, then rebuked them for their lack of faith. It was a test. In reality, that is when we learn the best—when we're in over our heads. Allowing staff to launch out into new water, taking a risk, is part of the test of their faith and mettle.

He Included Them

"After six days Jesus took with him Peter, James and John the brother of James, and led them up a high mountain by themselves. There he was transfigured before them" (Matt. 17:1–2).

Jesus gave some responsibilities to the seventy, some to the Twelve, and some special privileges to the three—Peter, James, and John. Some of the leaders in your church, both lay and professional staff, have more potential than others. To develop their potential to the maximum, you may need to give extra attention to some.

He Made Them His Friends

Jesus told his followers, "I no longer call you servants, because a servant does not know his master's business. Instead, I have called you friends, for everything that I learned from my Father I have made known to you" (John 15:15).

Some leaders adopt an arm's-length style of leadership and never develop the close camaraderie that inspires devoted loyalty. Jesus, the Son of God and Savior of the world, called mere mortals, fishermen with dirt under their fingernails, his friends. We can learn a great lesson here from the Master of supervision.

He Warned and Restored Them

Jesus warned his disciples that treacherous roads lay ahead. He warned them of the dangers of falling away. Although he boasted that he would never fall away, Peter denied the Lord three times. Yet, an angel told the women at the tomb, following the resurrection, "But go, tell his disciples *and Peter*, 'He is going ahead of you into Galilee. There you will see him, just as he told you'" (Mark 16:7, emphasis added).

Jesus wanted to make sure Peter was included in the group that would meet him in Galilee. When the Lord restored Peter, he gave him the task of feeding his sheep.

Staff members will not all perform perfectly. But our acceptance of them, even though they make mistakes, will build confidence in them and enable them to perform better in the future.

Keys to Good Supervision

Several years ago, an article appeared in *Business Courier* entitled, "What Employees Expect of the 'Ideal' Supervisor." The article dealt with the turnover of employees, why they come and go, and the bottom line involved several observations. "How much did I enjoy my boss? Was he motivating? Did she allow me to develop new skills? Or was he a jerk who cared only for the next promotion and was I the only unfortunate dupe to realize his boss made the huge mistake of having people report to this buffoon?"[7]

Some of those questions use harsh words. But what would your staff people say upon exiting from a position in which you were the supervisor? Think about the following ideas.

Communication

I will have more to say about communication in chapter 7. But for now, remember that so much of life begins and ends with good communication. Do it well, and you're on top of the world. Do it poorly, and everybody suffers.

Unfortunately, instead of developing the skills to be a good communicator, many senior pastors resort to top-down leadership. However, as President Dwight D. Eisenhower said, "You don't lead by hitting people over the head—that's assault, not leadership."[8]

Good communication, on the other hand, takes people, their skills, and their ideas into consideration. Abraham Lincoln was a master at getting other people to give their opinions and of listening to their ideas. In the end he made the decision, but he listened. One newspaperman wrote: "All (who) claim the personal acquaintance of Mr. Lincoln will agree that he is the very embodiment of good temper and affability. They will all concede that he has a kind word, an encouraging smile, a humorous remark for near all (who seek) his presence, and that but few, if any, emerge from his reception room without being strongly and favorably impressed with his general disposition."[9]

Top-Down Leadership

Why people resort to top-down leadership:

It's Traditional. Through the centuries, most leadership has been autocratic.

It's the Most Common. We have many books on various kinds of leadership, but the most common is still top-down.

It's the Easiest. You don't have to learn a new method of leadership when you bark orders.

It Comes Naturally. It seems built into our psyches to dominate people.

It Reflects the Depravity of Humankind. Satan's rebelled to get free of submitting to God the Father. He has been trying to motivate us to operate from a self-centered mode ever since.

Consultation

Closely allied with communication is consultation. Consulting with your staff builds their self-esteem as well as giving you the benefit of their thinking. Before making decisions that will affect the job responsibilities of a staff member, do him or her the honor of consultation.

Abraham Lincoln went through several generals in the Union Army before he found one who was effective enough to win the kinds of battles that ultimately defeated the Confederacy. John C. Fremont built a reputation as an explorer of the West and as a senator from the new state of California in 1850. But as commander of the army of the West during the Civil War, his performance was less than stellar.

When President Lincoln replaced him, the chief executive sent a letter to General Hunter, Fremont's successor, in which he wrote, "He (Fremont) is losing the confidence of men near him, whose support any man in his position must have to be successful." Lincoln added, "His cardinal mistake is that he isolates himself, and allows nobody to see him; and by which he does not know what is going on in the very matter he is dealing with."[10]

We can't afford to be in the dark about what is happening around us. One of the best ways to gain this knowledge is to consult with staff.

Delegation

An important lesson for every executive is to learn to delegate. Dwight L. Moody is credited with saying, "It is better to set ten men to work than to do the work of ten men."[11] In assessing the strengths and weaknesses of leaders, Warren Bennis and Burt

Nanus asserted that successful leaders lead with their strengths and learn from their weakness. In order to compensate for weakness, they learn to delegate.[12]

A colleague told me about an acquaintance who delegated by telling his subordinate not only what to do, but also exactly how he was to do it. Most people bristle at this kind of delegation. "You don't even try to control how people do their jobs," said Edgar Speer, chairman of US Steel. "There's no way to do that, furthermore, no purpose. Everyone does the job a different way, and they all want to show how well they can do it their way. The function of a supervisor is to analyze results rather than try to control how the job is done."[13]

Trust Their Ingenuity

Never tell people how to do things. Tell them what to do and they will surprise you with their ingenuity.

—George S. Patton

Affirmation

Giving positive feedback is one of the best things a senior pastor can do. An "attaboy" or "attagirl" at the right time is almost better than a raise in pay. Almost. A genuine attitude of encouragement toward others will almost inevitably reap better performance. We all like to be told we have done a good job.

When David McKenna became president of Asbury Theological Seminary, he asked five new faculty members, who had just completed their first semester of teaching at the seminary, "If you were president, what is the first thing you would do?"

He took copious notes as the first four gave him detailed responses. But when Dr. William Goold, professor of music, spoke, he said, "I'd study the law of gravity." McKenna's puzzled look encouraged him to continue. "In an institution like ours, the spirit of the place trickles down from top to bottom. That's why, if I were president, I'd be a student of the law of gravity."[14]

He was right. Attitudes are contagious. They do trickle down from the top.

Confrontation

In every human relationship, conflicts are bound to arise. Not all of them require confrontation. But when they do, the wise leader tries to handle it in a positive and constructive way. Sydney J. Harris, a writer for the Field Newspaper Syndicate, once wrote, "It is impossible to learn anything important about anyone until we get him or her to disagree with us; it is only in contradiction that character is disclosed. That is why autocratic employers usually remain so ignorant about the true nature of their subordinates."[15]

Don't let it be said of you that you did not listen, did not consult your staff, failed to delegate, failed to affirm, or shied away from confrontation. Handled wisely, these five things can enable you to become an effective supervisor.

Supervising Wisely

Dwight D. Eisenhower, thirty-fourth president of the United States, defined leadership as "the art of getting someone else to do something you want done because he wants to do it."[16] Supervising staff, while giving them a sense of accomplishment and helping them act because they want to and not because you told them to, requires some wisdom and finesse.

Persuade Rather Than Coerce

If you have to coerce people into doing things, you have abandoned leadership for dictatorship. God took the risk of giving the human family the freedom of choice. He could have made us robots that did his bidding without any choice on our part. But he obviously preferred to have individuals follow him because we want to do so.

Abraham Lincoln is a superb example of someone who believed in the power of persuasion. As a forty-one-year-old lawyer, he advised his listeners: "Discourage litigation. Persuade your neighbors to compromise whenever you can."[17] Speaking to the Springfield Washington Temperance Society in 1842, he said,

> When the conduct of men is designed to be influenced, *persuasion*, kind, unassuming persuasion, should ever be adopted. It is an old and true maxim, that a "drop of honey catches more flies than a gallon of gall." So with men. If you would win a man to your cause, *first* convince him that you are his sincere friend. Therein is a drop of honey that catches his heart. . . . On the contrary, assume to dictate to his judgment, or to command his action, or to mark him as one to be shunned and despised, and he will retreat within himself, close all the avenues to his head and heart; and tho' your cause be naked truth itself . . . you shall no more be able to [reach] him, than to penetrate the hard shell of a tortoise with a rye straw.[18]

Coercion means you have run out of good ideas and have resorted to top-down leadership. Persuasion means you respect your staff persons enough to engage their minds and hearts.

Encourage Innovation

If there were no innovation, life would go on as it has always been, with no new products, methods, or ideas. Obviously, too much change, implemented too fast, can be detrimental. But encouraging your staff members to innovate is a great complement to their creativity and resourcefulness.

No Desire to Lead

A true but safe leader is likely to be one who has no desire to lead, but is forced into a position of leadership by the inward pressure of the Holy Spirit and the press of the external situation. . . .
I believe . . . that the man who is ambitious to lead is disqualified as a leader. The true leader will have no desire to lord it over God's heritage, but will be humble, gentle, self-sacrificing and altogether as ready to follow as to lead, when the Spirit makes it clear that a wiser and more gifted man than himself has appeared.

—A. W. Tozer

A true leader "does not wait for things to happen, but makes them happen. He is a self-starter and is always on the lookout for improved methods. He will be willing to test new ideas."[19]

Help Them Find Their "Fit"

I have known some highly successful senior pastors who were able to shift roles among their staff members without hiring new individuals because they saw that one person was gifted in a certain area. The new role was a better fit for the staff person than the role for which he or she was originally hired.

This fits with Oswald Sanders' comment that "leadership is the ability to recognize the special abilities and limitations of others, combined with the capacity to fit each one into the job where he will do his best."[20] It is actually a compliment to staff members when the senior pastor recognizes their gifts and employs them.

President Lincoln asked Salmon P. Chase to be his Secretary of the Treasury, even though Chase had been an opponent in the presidential election of 1860. The two often clashed over various matters, leading Chase to submit his resignation more than once. Lincoln refused to accept it until the fourth time, in June 1864, when Lincoln finally had enough. Later, however, Lincoln appointed Chase as the new chief justice of the Supreme Court.

Some people protested this move, and Lincoln responded publicly by saying: "Chase is a very able man. He is a very ambitious man and I think on the subject of the presidency a little insane. He has not always behaved very well lately and people say to me, 'Now is the time to *crush him out*.' Well, I'm not in favor of crushing anybody out! If there is anything that a man can do and do it well, I say let him do it. Give him a chance."[21]

Listen

If you want people to take you seriously, then take them seriously. One of the best ways to do this is to listen. News anchor Diane Sawyer, who has interviewed hundreds of people, said, "I think the one lesson I have learned is that there is no substitute for paying attention."[22]

Through the wise man, wisdom personified speaks: "Blessed is the man who listens to me, watching daily at my doors, waiting at my doorway. For whoever finds me finds life and receives favor from the LORD" (Prov. 8:34–35). How do we find wisdom in order to listen to it? One way is to listen to others. We never learn anything while we are talking; we only learn when we are listening.

Your staff members have worthwhile things to say. They are likely closer to some members of your congregation than you are. They are also likely closer to some ministries and situations in your church than you are. You cannot possibly be everywhere and hear everything (nor do you want to!). But staff members who are paying attention can help you be better informed—provided you are paying attention to them.

Be Consistent

Be the same person with your staff as you are with your board. Be the same person with your staff as you are when you greet people in the church foyer. It's true that you relate to different people in different ways. But the importance of consistency in how you treat people cannot be overstated.

The Eisenhower Center in Abilene, Kansas, where our thirty-fourth president spent his boyhood, said it received very few requests for recordings of Oval Office conversations between Eisenhower and many government leaders. This phenomenon stands in contrast to the popularity of tape recordings of former presidents Richard Nixon, Lyndon Johnson, and John F. Kennedy.

Mack Teasley, assistant director at the center, said, "The tapes show me that Eisenhower was the same person operating in the Oval Office as he was in a public appearance or at a press conference. There's nothing earth-shattering in the tapes."[23]

Consistency is a quality of integrity of character.

The Voice and the Touch

When Max DePree first saw his grandson, born three months prematurely, wires were running from the baby's body, which was hardly as long as DePree's hand. The baby's father had left his mother when she was expecting the child. So the senior nurse came to DePree and told him that for the next three months, he was going to be the surrogate father. When he visited, he was to put his hands in the incubator, rub the baby's back, and talk to him at the same time. She said, "It's very important that he get your voice and touch together. Premature babies especially need that for security."

So DePree did that for three months, putting in his hand and gently rubbing the little back and talking to his grandson. DePree said, "That is a good picture of what leadership is. Leadership involves getting the voice and the touch together."[24]

Supervising staff members involves getting the voice and the touch together. It involves consistency, listening, persuasion, helping staff find their niche, and encouraging innovation.

Action Steps

1. Think back over your recent conversations with staff. How much have you talked and how much have you listened? What adjustments do you need to make in that ratio?
2. This chapter lists several reasons why supervision often falls short. How many of them apply to your supervision in the past year? What adjustments do you need to make?
3. What methods have you used recently to affirm your staff members? What new methods of affirmation will you try?

7 COMMUNICATION
KEEPING THE LINES OPEN

Communicating with staff members—both speaking and listening—will keep the lines open for effective ministry.

Nothing in life is more important than the ability to communicate effectively.
—GERALD R. FORD

Pastor Ben sat before the church's board with fear and trembling. He remembered reading somewhere in the church's bylaws that they were not supposed to call a meeting without the pastor's approval. Unfortunately, the pastor was on vacation. Ben was beginning to understand what it might be like to stand in front of a firing squad.

It all began with a friendly enough invitation to meet with the board on a Tuesday night. He had completed two years of effective service (at least in his own mind), working with the church's junior and senior high teens. Spending at least twenty hours a week in youth ministry while he finished his degree at the nearby college had been a very satisfying experience—until tonight.

Thinking they might want to commend him for his service since they were near the end of the church year, or perhaps even ask him to come to work full-time once he finished his degree, he was totally unprepared for what unfolded. The leader of the board brought out a list of all the things Ben had done wrong in the past two years. As the list grew, Ben's heart sank a little further. He wished the floor would open up and swallow him.

He sat and listened. He wanted to defend himself, but he had the feeling that it was useless. When they came to the end of the list, the board asked for his resignation.

Where was the senior pastor? "If he were here, surely he would speak up on my behalf," Ben thought. "Or would he?" Come to think of it, most of the charges were true or at least held a grain of truth. On the other hand, nobody had ever taught him to be a youth pastor. He had received zero mentoring during his two years. And, what hurt Ben deeply, the more he thought about it, was that he and the senior pastor had almost no relationship.

Scenarios like the one outlined above have occurred in far too many church board meetings across the years. No wonder many staff members have short tenures. We could avoid a great deal of it if we had better communication.

Short Supply of Effective Communication?

Why is effective communication in such short supply in some circles? We have computers, cell phones, wireless capabilities; we can talk; we can text; we can tweet. Why don't we do a better job?

Making Assumptions

A man, walking down the street, saw a home owner struggling with a washing machine in the doorway of his home. He offered to help, and the home owner gladly accepted his offer. They struggled for a few minutes and made no progress. Exhausted, they stopped and looked at each other.

Wiping sweat off his forehead, the passerby said, "Man, at this rate, we're never going to get this machine in there."

The home owner took a step back and said, "In there? I'm trying to move it out!"

The passerby, for all his good intentions, assumed he knew what was going on, but the opposite was true.

Trust

Never assume that you fully understand . . . use the power of questions to learn more.

—Brian Tracy

I have known supervising pastors, as well as supervisors in other fields, who made assumptions about what their staff members did and didn't know. One assistant pastor said, "It happens every few weeks. I come into the office and the senior pastor will be gone. When I ask his administrative assistant, she says, 'Oh, yes, he has a meeting out of town with a district committee.' Or, 'He and his wife decided they needed a day away.'"

The assistant pastor added, "It's none of my business what he does with his time away from the office, but it's a little unnerving to discover he's gone when I didn't even know if I was on call or not."

Howard Hendricks used to tell his seminary students, "Men, if it's a mist in the pulpit, it will be a fog in the pew."[1] He was talking about preaching, of course, but you can also leave your staff in a fog if you assume they know things they don't.

Leaving Others in the Dark

Closely aligned with making assumptions is leaving staff members in the dark. I have known pastors who seemed to take the attitude, "I'm in charge. I don't have to explain every decision I make. They don't have to know everything."

Even if that's true, why would you not want your staff to be well-informed? Red Auerbach, who coached the Boston Celtics to nine National Basketball Association championships between 1956 and 1966, said, "It's not what you tell your players that counts. It's what they hear."[2]

He was talking about the gap that sometimes exists between what we say and what others hear. But if you are not even telling them, it's certain they will remain in the dark. If you're leaving them in the dark, they're going to hear all the stuff that's circulating. Without being well-informed, they won't know if it's true or not. Your staff can be your strongest allies—if they know what's happening. Don't leave them in the dark.

Listening Instead of Talking

The flip side of leaving your staff in the dark is talking too much. Contrary to popular opinion, communication is at least as much about listening as it is talking, probably more so. The larger your church and the more staff you have, the farther you tend to be from the front lines. Consequently, listening becomes even more important.

Listening has to be intentional. During your staff meetings, be sure you take time to listen to each person. It's easy to give orders, dispense assignments, tell people what to do. It's more challenging—and more profitable—to listen. People will tell staff members things they won't tell you. You don't have to know everything that's going on, but it's important to be informed.

Many factors will work against being a good listener. Listening takes time, and you will feel that you don't have enough time. Listening takes energy, and you will feel yours draining away as some people

The Gift of Listening

Use the gift of listening. Somehow this is very difficult for all of us. We talk, many times, because we think we need to say something. Listening is hard.

—Billy Graham

talk. With e-mails, paperwork accumulating on your desk, along with demands from your district or region, you will think you have information overload as it is. Why should you ask for more input?

I have known a pastor or two so proud that they didn't think their staff members could tell them anything. But remember what Scripture says: "Be quick to listen, slow to speak" (James 1:19).

"The Words of My Mouth"

I quote Psalm 19:14 everyday: "Let the words of my mouth, and the meditation of my heart, be acceptable in thy sight, O LORD, my strength, and my redeemer" (KJV). It's an important prayer because words have the power to bless, but also to blast. They can build up or they can tear down. They can affirm or they can denigrate. They can encourage or they can discourage, compliment or insult, express love or disdain.

Words matter. They matter a great deal. Jesus taught us, "For out of the overflow of the heart the mouth speaks. The good man brings good things out of the good stored up in him, and the evil man brings evil things out of the evil stored up in him" (Matt. 12:34–35).

You probably know people who spew evil or at least discouragement with almost every breath. You probably also know people whose words are tender, positive, and healing. They bring a sense of well-being to your mind and heart.

James had a great deal to say about the use, misuse, and abuse of the tongue. He even went so far as to say, "If anyone considers himself religious and yet does not keep a tight rein on his tongue, he deceives himself and his religion is worthless" (James 1:26). Imagine having God say, "Your religion was worthless, all because you did not keep a tight rein on your tongue."

Think of the damage a loose, undisciplined tongue can do. I have known it to create havoc in church circles. Pastors are not immune. In fact, we may be even more susceptible to lack of discipline because we talk so much.

A Native American attended a church in which it became obvious to him that the preacher was not well-prepared. To compensate for lack of spiritual depth in the sermon, the minister pounded the pulpit and raised his voice.

After the sermon, someone asked the Native American what he thought of the service. He summed up his opinion this way: "High wind. Big thunder. No rain."

Staff members are not immune from undisciplined tongues either. Vicious rumors can circulate and take on a life of their own within the walls of the church offices. How sad that some people's lives have been destroyed because one or more of God's children did not keep a tight rein on their tongues.

James went on to make some vivid comparisons. He said, "When we put bits into the mouths of horses to make them obey us, we can turn the whole animal. Or take ships as an example. Although they are so large and are driven by strong winds, they are steered by a very small rudder wherever the pilot wants to go" (James 3:3–4).

Then James went on to make the application: "Likewise the tongue is a small part of the body, but it makes great boasts. Consider what a great forest is set on fire by a small spark. The tongue also is a fire, a world of evil among the parts of the body. It corrupts the whole person, sets the whole course of his life on fire, and is itself set on fire by hell" (James 3:5–6).

James also shows the power of the tongue for both good and evil. He said, "With the tongue we praise our Lord and Father, and with it we curse men, who have been made in God's likeness. Out of the same mouth come praise and cursing. My brothers, this should not be. Can both fresh water and salt water flow from the same spring? My brothers, can a fig tree bear olives, or a grapevine bear figs? Neither can a salt spring produce fresh water" (James 3:9–12).

We can use our tongues to bless and encourage staff members, or we can use them to bring discouragement and dismay. I have known staff members who would have performed their ministries with much more effectiveness and excellence if their senior pastors had paid attention and given a few compliments along the way.

Communicating with Parishioners

Communicating with staff is no substitute for communicating with your laypersons. I suggest a few ways to communicate effectively in ninety minutes a day:

- Spend one hour in one-to-one ministry.
- Spend fifteen minutes on correspondence.
- Spend fifteen minutes on phone calls.
- Spend fifteen minutes using social media—Facebook, Twitter, etc.

Jesus was a master at drawing the best out of people. We remember some of the disciples for their boastfulness and competitiveness. Yet Jesus found ways to praise them. We remember that they argued about who was the greatest in the kingdom. Yet Jesus saw great worth in them.

On one occasion, he said, "You are the salt of the earth" (Matt. 5:13). In other words, "You are the kind of people who can give this world a better flavor. As salt keeps meat from spoiling, you are the kind of people who can preserve society by your influence."

He also told them, "You are the light of the world" (Matt. 5:14). In other words, "You are the kind of people who can light the way for others to find the pathway to God. You can enlighten them and brighten their lives." Further he said, "Let your light shine before men, that they may see your good deeds and praise your Father in heaven" (Matt. 5:16).

As we affirm and encourage our staff members, we will improve their self-worth and improve their value to the church.

Effective Communication

If you think communication is simple or easy, you may want to reexamine what planet you're living on. It should be easy, right? After all, it's primarily just talking and listening.

Gary McIntosh told about a trained investigator who mingled with the crowds at Grand Central Station in New York City at the height of vacation season. He asked a simple question of ten people. The question: "What is your destination?" People gave him the following responses:

- Protestant.
- Mind your own business.
- I'm a shoe salesman.
- Home, if I can find my wife.
- I'm learning to be a mail clerk.
- Checkers.
- Shut your mouth!

- I don't know you.
- Hoboken.
- I believe in faith, hope, and charity.[3]

We could probably attribute the confusion in the previous example to all the noise in a busy place like Grand Central Station. Perhaps some people simply did not understand the question. But that does not excuse all our failures to communicate.

Tom Mullins contends that all communication has five basic elements:

1. What you think you want to say.
2. What you actually say.
3. What the other person thinks he or she heard you say.
4. The other person's response to what he or she heard you say.
5. Your reaction to his or her interpretation of what you said.[4]

Actually, according to research at Brigham Young University, the content of your communication, that is, the meaning of the words you say, contributes only 7 percent of your communication impact. In addition to content, you have to think about the visual component—how you look and behave. Your body language contributes 55 percent of your communication impact. The auditory component, how you sound and tone of voice, makes up the other 38 percent.[5]

How we communicate with others is vitally important. Tim Stafford says, "Our speech is never truly accidental. If you listen to someone talk for long enough, you will know what kind of person he or she is. Careless words may reveal more than carefully planned speeches. A mouth opens, and out pops a heart." He went on to say, "Your talk is a rudder by which you can steer your life."[6]

We all use words to talk to people, but talking is not the same thing as communicating. Real communicating is not just conveying information; it's getting through to people. As senior pastors, we communicate with our staff members in one of several ways.

Attention

Paying attention to people is like paying them a sincere compliment. If you communicate attentiveness to your staff members when they talk, they are more likely to listen to you.

Giving them attention is not the same as pampering them. Take them seriously; make eye contact; let them know you have time for them; and create an atmosphere that says, "I am not anxious to get on with my other duties. You have my full attention."

Antagonism

Treating your staff members as antagonists is inexcusable—unless, of course, they are antagonists. Occasionally, you may be unfortunate enough to encounter a staff member who irritates you. Sometimes they will be outright antagonistic, even to the point of working behind your back to undercut authority. When that happens, you have serious problems that go beyond communication difficulties.

Yet poor communication may lead to such problems. If a staff member acts distant or seems to be avoiding

Overcoming Antagonism

E. Stanley Jones said the way to overcome antagonism is to "begin to move toward others in love. God moved toward you in gracious, outgoing love, and you move toward others in that same outgoing love."

you, ask yourself if you have failed to communicate properly. The reasons for such behavior on the part of a staff member may be many. Just be sure it isn't because you have held him or her at arm's length and failed to communicate.

Apathy

Occasionally I have known senior pastors who communicated an attitude that said, "I don't care." They seemed detached, out of touch, and uninvolved in the lives of their staff members. You cannot be effective if you allow yourself to become apathetic.

An effective senior pastor cares about everything and everybody. You cannot be involved in everything—that's why you have a staff. But you have to care. What does it communicate to the director of children's ministry if you come across as disinterested in his or her area of the church? What if it's obvious that you are extremely interested in evangelism, but couldn't care less about how the youth ministry is doing?

You may have areas of the church that spark your enthusiasm more than others, but don't fall prey to apathy.

Affirmation

I will have more to say about affirmation in chapter 10, but remember that "few things in the world are more powerful than a positive push—a smile. A word of optimism and hope, a 'you can do it!' when things are tough."[7]

Skitch Henderson, renowned musical conductor and founder of the New York Pops, said, "I watch the public like a hawk. If I see boredom, I worry. You can tell by the applause: There's perfunctory applause, there's light applause, and then there's real applause. When it's right, applause sounds like vanilla ice cream with chocolate sauce."[8]

Entertainers crave applause. All of us appreciate affirmation, a little verbal applause now and then.

Improving Communication

There is no magic formula for good communication between you and your staff members. However, good principles of communication work in a variety of settings. Here are a few tips that might make your interactions more effective.

Design Clear Job Descriptions

I wrote about job descriptions in chapter 2, so there is no need to be repetitive here, except to emphasize the importance of clear job descriptions as a vital part of communication. How will your staff members know what is expected of them unless they have it in clear, written form?

Revising the job description from time to time makes sense. If your church is growing, the ministry in a given area may become more complicated. You may observe strengths in your staff person that you hadn't noticed before—weaknesses, too—and you may want to adjust the job description accordingly.

Hold Regular Staff Meetings

Some pastors love staff meetings; others hate them. They see them as an intrusion on their other responsibilities. But when you agreed to become a senior pastor, you agreed to become a supervisor. Supervision includes regular communication with staff persons and consistent staff meetings are a good way to accomplish this.

How will you communicate your vision and values if you have no venue, like a staff meeting, to accomplish it? How will you communicate leadership principles (also part of your responsibility) if you do not have meetings during which that can be accomplished?

In addition, staff meetings provide opportunities for regular interaction, fellowship, camaraderie, and building a team spirit. We vary in our need for such fellowship. Some staff members will relish it; others will tolerate it. But everybody needs it. Don't let their aversion to meeting deter you from doing what you know you should do.

Meet One-on-One with Staff Members

Staff meetings do not take the place of one-on-one meetings with the various members of your staff. You may not need to meet every week. Or you may find it important to meet that often. You can design these to fit your situation.

But regular one-on-one meetings with staff members gives them an opportunity to voice concerns they may not feel free to bring up in the larger group. They also give you an opportunity to deal with issues that should be handled one-on-one and not in a group setting. If you only meet one-on-one when there's a problem, such meetings take on the tone of "being called to the principal's office." It can set other staff persons to whispering, "I wonder why the pastor wanted to meet alone with Bill? Is he in trouble?" Not good for morale.

Manage by Wandering Around

This phrase—and this method of supervision—was popularized by Tom Peters and Robert Waterman in their 1982 book *In Search of Excellence*. It simply means that instead of directing the church's activities and supervising staff from behind your desk, you get up and wander around—with purpose, of course—and visit your staff members in their own setting. You may want to conduct one-on-one meetings in their office occasionally to vary the routine.

A colleague used to say, "You can't run this thing from behind a desk." He meant you need to get out and see for yourself what's really happening. This kind of informal supervision communicates warmth, a sense that you care about what's happening in their world, and a sense that you are interested in every aspect of the church—which, of course, you are.

Practice HOT Communication

Hans Finzel recommends HOT communication, meaning Honest, Open, and Transparent. He adds, "Nothing happens until people talk."[9] Being open and honest with each other, transparent about ideas and feelings, can keep the lines of communication open.

As a senior pastor, being open to new ideas and receptive to out-of-the-box thinking can give you a great deal of credibility with your staff. You may not be able to approve every new idea, but being open speaks volumes.

Being Honest

Each time you are honest, you propel yourself toward greater success. Each time you lie, even a little white lie, you push yourself toward failure.

—John Mason

An Unfortunate Casualty

Pastor Ben, who sat speechless in front of the church's board, did submit his resignation. When the senior pastor returned, he did nothing to defend Ben. Neither did he offer any encouragement. In fact, it would have been better if he had said nothing. What he did say only twisted the knife more deeply: "I could see it coming. But I knew you would never change."

Ben is no longer in church ministry. He has found a different career and serves as a faithful layperson in a local church, where he does his best to encourage staff members. He has risen above his experience and has not allowed it to poison his mind against senior pastors. He has shown great maturity in overcoming a very hurtful experience.

As senior pastors, let's be sure that no more "Bens" become casualties. As someone said, "Casualness can lead to casualties." Senior pastors who are too casual, not paying enough attention, and not providing the kind of encouragement staff members need may contribute to such casualties.

But, as the New Testament writer said, "We are confident of better things in your case" (Heb. 6:9). With God's help and direction, you will become the kind of senior pastor who develops staff, encourages them, and forms a dynamic team for God and the church.

Action Steps

1. Think about the communication level with your staff. What procedures are in place to inform the staff of your absence?
2. Think about the last time you experienced a mix-up in communication among your staff members, whether you were included in the mix-up or not. How could that have been avoided?
3. What plan do you follow regarding staff meetings? How could this be improved?

8

Coaching
Giving Effective Feedback

Coaching your staff members will enable them to grow and will add value to your church.

Someday people in the church will recognize that effective leadership is coaching, and that the most effective Christian leaders—and the most effective Christians—must be effective coaches.
—Gary R. Collins

Pastor Jim listened to his youth pastor talk about his goals and ambitions. Since coming to First Church two years earlier, young Pastor Fred had seen the youth group double and many young people had made first-time commitments to Christ. In addition, these young people had influenced their parents and, in some cases, the parents began attending First Church. Several of them had also made commitments to Christ.

But now Fred was talking about his desire to be a senior pastor some day. He was not unhappy as a youth pastor. In fact, he found it very fulfilling. But he also dreamed of the day he would lead his own church. He felt he was developing a message for adults as well as young people.

As Fred talked, Jim had to admit to himself that the young man's preaching had matured. On the occasions when Jim was on vacation or out of the pulpit for some other reason, Fred had done a good job. Unlike the previous youth pastor who had embarrassed

Jim with his silliness in the pulpit, Fred was able to make the switch from being solely a youth-oriented speaker to an adult-oriented speaker.

When Fred paused and seemed to be waiting for feedback, Jim said, "Tell me, Fred, what do you think you need to do in order to be ready to lead a church?"

Fred admitted he wasn't ready just yet. But it was a goal he wanted to reach.

"Well, Fred, let me be honest. My default role is supervisor; you understand that. But if you are willing, I would like to put on my coaching hat. Perhaps together, we can figure out how to get from here to there. I knew when you came that you probably wouldn't stay forever. I'm very pleased with your work, but I also see your potential and would like to help you develop it."

Fred agreed and they determined they would set up regular times to talk about what it would take to help Fred get from where he was to the place where he could become the lead pastor of a church.

Roadblocks to Coaching

When many people think of coaching, they imagine a football or basketball coach, maybe a Little League or soccer coach. That certainly is one kind of coaching. But the kind of coaching that helps a person reach his or her potential is different from athletic coaching.

A Different Kind of Coach

A coach in the sense I'm talking about would be better understood if you do not picture a man or woman standing on the sidelines, whistle at the ready, encouraging (or yelling at) a group of players. Rather, picture Cinderella's pumpkin coach. Think of it as a vehicle of conveyance. Maybe a Greyhound coach would be more to your liking. But think about a vehicle to carry a person from one place to another.

Coaching Can Be Learned

Coaching will become the model of leaders in the future. Coaches train, mentor, and empower. I am certain that leadership can be learned and that terrific coaches . . . facilitate learning.

—Warren Bennis

A personal coach is someone who accepts others where they are and works with them to help them arrive at a destination.

The Answer Man

Several roadblocks can sidetrack the coaching process. One is when the coach feels like he or she has to have a solution for every problem that arises. Preachers by default have answers. Our training has taught us to know the Scriptures and that God's Word gives us the answers to life's problems. A little experience along the way has taught us how people have made poor choices that resulted in shattered lives. Our training prepares us to help people put their lives back together by giving them time-tested answers.

However, that does not help the person grow. When we have to think through our own problems, work through our issues, and discover the answers within ourselves, the result is not only a better solution; it is tremendous growth. A coach learns to stifle the impulse to blurt out an answer. A better solution is to ask a question that will cause our friend to think more deeply or differently about a problem.

The Discomfort of Silence

This leads to another potential roadblock: the discomfort of silence. What happens when you ask a question and the person just sits there? Answer: it gets very quiet. Few of us enjoy absolute quiet unless we are alone. Silence between two people who are supposed to be having a conversation makes most of us uncomfortable.

But that silence can prove to be a catalyst that leads to better insight. After a period of silence, a person will often make a statement that reveals considerable thought and self-discovery. If not—if their next comment is not helpful—another question may be appropriate.

Silence can be powerful. When we interrupt the silence with our own observations, we may short-circuit the process that forces the other person to come up with his or her own solutions. Letting the silence soak in and allowing time for the other person to think deeply about the question you just asked can be much more helpful than making one more statement.

Active Listening

Another component that adds great value to the coaching process is active listening. We said a great deal about listening in the previous chapter. But briefly, let me further emphasize that not talking is not the same as listening. Active listening involves great attentiveness. It involves focusing entirely on the other person, hearing everything he or she has to say.

Actively listening to others is a way to connect with them. Paul J. Meyer pointed out, "If you want the other man's attention, first give him yours! If you listen, he will tell you all you will ever need to know about himself."[1]

When you actively listen to someone, you pay him or her a great compliment. In fact, the feeling of being listened to is so close to the feeling of being loved that most people cannot tell the difference.

Listening

One of the problems with listening is that it's often mistaken for doing nothing.

—Robert E. Logan and Sherilyn Carlton

Mister Encouragement

Barnabas is an example of a great coach. Although that terminology was not used in his day, he exemplified it.

When he was born on the island of Cyprus, his parents named him Joseph, a name held in high esteem among the Jewish people. As young Joseph grew, he met the followers of Jesus. They introduced him to the Christian way, which he accepted wholeheartedly. His Christian friends gradually noticed something different about Joseph. Whenever they were around him, they felt better. He always seemed to know the right things to say. He was happy and helpful and made others feel happy too. So they gave him a new name—Barnabas—which means "Son of Encouragement." Throughout his life, he lived up to his name.

A Positive Person

You may know some people who are not like Barnabas. The more you are around them, the more depressed you become. When you are in their presence, you feel a heavy weight on your shoulders. They're the kind of people who can brighten a whole room just by leaving it! Such people often find fault with others. They may be critical or pessimistic.

Not Barnabas. People enjoyed being around him. I heard about a little child who prayed a wonderful prayer, "Lord, make all the bad people good. And Lord, please make all the good people nice."

Barnabas had the ability to make goodness attractive. Nobody wants to be around those who will discourage them. Barnabas was a positive person who knew how to encourage others, which is one of the reasons he made a great coach.

A Bridge Builder

When Saul (later known as Paul) went to Jerusalem from Damascus, he wanted to meet the apostles. But the believers in Jerusalem were afraid of Saul. Their mood was to hold him off at arm's length. After all, not only was he a relatively new convert, he had a history of persecuting believers. They could have rejected Paul.

Nevertheless, Barnabas became Saul's friend, went to bat for Saul, and recommended him to the apostles. "He told them how Saul on his journey had seen the Lord and that the Lord had spoken to him, and how in Damascus he had preached fearlessly in the name of Jesus" (Acts 9:27). It could have been a crucial turning point in sending Saul in the other direction. Instead, the church welcomed him, and Christianity has never been the same. All because Barnabas knew how to build bridges and bring people together, an admirable quality in a coach.

The Right Person in the Right Place

Later, Christianity spread north to Antioch. Many people turned to the Lord. Since it was a new region, the church in Jerusalem needed a sensitive person to investigate. They sent Barnabas, the positive, kindhearted encourager. Luke described it this way: "When [Barnabas] arrived and saw the evidence of the grace of God, he was glad and encouraged them all to remain true to the Lord with all their hearts. He was a good man, full of the Holy Spirit and faith, and a great number of people were brought to the Lord" (Acts 11:23–24).

"That's a great description of a coach: one who is called alongside to encourage, prepare, equip and help others succeed. Coaching is a biblical role."[2]

When Barnabas arrived in Antioch, he saw that some of the new believers were Gentiles. Some people would have been skeptical, thinking God would only work with the Jews. Barnabas was quick to see God's Spirit at work. He also saw that these new believers needed someone who would understand this unique movement of God's Spirit. He thought of Saul of Tarsus, so he went to Tarsus, found Saul, and brought him back.

Barnabas had the ability to find the right person for the right job and see God's kingdom advance. This is an admirable quality in a coach. Although the person being coached needs to determine the direction and the destination, a wise coach has the ability to spot talent, skill, and giftedness that will fit in the right place.

Shaping a Champion

When the church at Antioch decided to send out the first missionary team, the people chose Barnabas and Saul. I say, "the people chose," but in reality, it was the Holy Spirit who said, "'Set apart for me Barnabas and Saul for the work to which I have called them.' So after they had fasted and prayed, they placed their hands on them and sent them off" (Acts 13:2–3).

As the missionary venture proceeded, an interesting shift in leadership occurred. On the island of Cyprus, their immediate destination after leaving Antioch, "the proconsul, an intelligent man, sent for Barnabas and Saul because he wanted to hear the word of God." Barnabas is the first name listed. From Paphos, a port on the west coast of Cyprus, "Paul and his companions sailed to Perga in Pamphylia" (Acts 13:13). Barnabas was undoubtedly a part of the group, but Luke did not mention his name. While in the city of Antioch of Pisidia, the group ministered in the Jewish synagogue. But when they departed the synagogue one day, Luke wrote, "As Paul and Barnabas were leaving the synagogue . . ." (Acts 13:42). From that point, Paul is always mentioned first.

Barnabas not only knew how to build bridges and relationships, but he knew how to spot a person with gifts for ministry and take potential leaders under his wing. He also knew how to withdraw graciously and let his protégé step to the front. Barnabas never became as well-known as Paul, but where would Paul have been if Barnabas had not served as his sponsor, colleague, and coach?

A Second Chance

Barnabas also had the ability to lift those who had fallen. For some reason, Mark, who had begun the first missionary journey with Barnabas and Saul, turned back at Perga and returned to Jerusalem. This irritated Paul, who refused to consider Mark when it came time to put together a team for a second missionary venture. However, Barnabas believed in young Mark and took him along on his second trip to Cyprus (Acts 15:39).

Years later, Paul changed his mind about Mark. He wrote to Timothy, "Get Mark and bring him with you, because he is helpful to me in my ministry" (2 Tim. 4:11). What happened to Mark that caused Paul to change his opinion of the young man who had "deserted them in Pamphylia" (Acts 15:38)? Why was he now "profitable" to Paul (KJV)?

Could it be that Barnabas coached and mentored Mark on their missionary trip? Barnabas, the son of encouragement, knew how to encourage those who had fallen and help them try again.

Understand Coaching

I defined coaching earlier as a vehicle to help people travel from where they are to where they want to be in a meaningful, purposeful way. It may be helpful to consider what coaching is *not*.

Not Counseling

Coaching is not the same as counseling. Counseling tends to focus on the past. Something has happened that profoundly influences the way a person thinks and acts. Counseling seeks to discover what happened and how the person can experience healing. In the best-case scenario, the person overcomes a past event or influence to the point where it no longer has a detrimental effect on current behavior. The person experiences sufficient healing that the present and future are not held hostage.

Coaching, on the other hand, is much more about the future. Coaching begins where a person is and determines what future point he or she wants to reach. A coach may ask questions that enable a person to see more clearly what is wanted and how to get there. Coaching focuses on forward movement, agreed-upon goals, and intermediate steps.

Coaching "honors the other person as the expert in his or her life and work and believes that the person is creative and resourceful."[3]

Not Consulting

A consultant is a person who comes across as an expert. Consultants typically have a predetermined set of principles and strategies. They may even have a model as to how you should approach the problem or problems you face. A consultant is likely to have "the answer" to the situation. Although they may use assessment tools and engage in some analysis, they bring a solution that fits their model rather than necessarily fitting the situation.

Coaching on the other hand sees the senior pastor as the expert. A coach draws on people's understanding, not only of where they are, but where they want to go. A coach believes he or she holds the key to get from here to there. The coach's job is to assist people in determining the best path to take, the best methods to use, and the best way to answer the questions they have. Rather than starting with a preconceived model, the coach helps people design a plan that fits the situation.

Distinctions between Coaching and Counseling

Coaching
- Action
- Present to future focus
- Create and design
- Expertise lies with person being coached
- Promotes discovery
- Future possibilities
- What and how
- Proactive
- Achievement
- Joy

Counseling (traditional model)
- Understanding and issues
- Past to present focus
- Repair and resolve
- Expertise lies within counselor
- Gives answers and advice
- Past events
- Why
- Curative
- Healing
- Happiness

—Linda Miller

"Coaching is partnering with others as you rely on Christ's teachings and presence, focusing on what the person wants to address, encouraging intentional action, and reviewing to reach clear agreements about the actions."[4]

The Positive Nature of Coaching

So what is coaching? It is helping persons focus on their potential rather than settling for where they are or where they have always been.

Miami Dolphins football coach Don Shula entered a hospital room where the patient, Mike Westhoff, special teams coach for the Dolphins, was recovering from bone cancer. Mike thanked him for coming. Shula asked how he was doing. He answered, "Oh, okay," but the look in his sunken eyes told a different story.

After a long pause, Shula leaned in, his jaw close to the face of the patient.

"Listen, Mike. I need you in training camp in July—on the field, ready to go. We're going all the way this year."

Later Westhoff said of Shula, "I thought he would tuck me in, but he didn't. He treated me the way I could be, not the way I was."[5]

That's what coaches do. They focus on potential. The German writer Johann Wolfgang Von Goethe said, "Treat people as if they were what they ought to be, and you help them become what they are capable of becoming."[6] He could have been describing a coach.

Coaching is also empowering people and enhancing what they do. The apostle Paul wrote many messages to young men like Timothy and Titus that empowered them to be all they could be. Someone might argue that Paul was not coaching; he was giving instructions.

But these instructions were not intended to define their lifetime goals nor to dictate their paths; rather Paul endeavored to give them life principles that empowered them to fulfill their destiny and reach their potential.

For instance, he wrote to Timothy, "Train yourself to be godly. For physical training is of some value, but godliness has value for all things, holding promise for both the present life and the life to come" (1 Tim. 4:7–8).

He also told Timothy, "Do not neglect your gift, which was given you through a prophetic message when the body of elders laid their hands on you" (1 Tim. 4:14). He urged the young man, "Fan into flame the gift of God, which is in you through the laying on of my hands. For God did not give us a spirit of timidity, but a spirit of power, of love and of self-discipline" (2 Tim. 1:6–7).

Sometimes the people we are trying to coach are their own worst enemies because of their low self-esteem. Somewhere along the way, they began to believe people or influences in their lives that told them they were limited, unable to fulfill their destiny, or deficient in some other way. By empowering them to believe in their own ability, along with the power of God within them, we encourage them to become all they can be.

Working through Coaching Stages

Robert Logan and Sherilyn Carlton have boiled the coaching process down to five stages:

1. Relate—Establish the coaching relationship and the agenda for your time together.

2. Reflect—Discover and explore key issues.
3. Refocus—Determine priorities and action steps.
4. Resource—Provide support and encouragement.
5. Review—Evaluate, celebrate, and revise your plans.[7]

Relating

Relating operates on the premise that coaching is, first and foremost, a relationship. Having said that, one should not be fooled into thinking it is simple. Relationships can be complicated. They demand time and effort. So establishing the basis for the relationship at the outset is extremely important.

Does your staff person want to grow in a certain area? Does he or she want to reach a certain goal? Remember, it's all about this person's agenda and what he or she wants to work on throughout the coming weeks. Listening is a major part of the relationship, and I discussed that earlier in this chapter. But let me remind you again: Listening is hard work and it demands your complete attention.

Relationships

Without relationships we would be incredibly lonely and isolated. As J. A. Holmes said, "It is well to remember that the entire population of the universe, with one trifling exception, is composed of others."

Asking questions is also part of the relationship. Asking questions is a discipline that helps the coach overcome the tendency to offer advice. It is very easy for us to jump in with some advice or a solution. Asking a question that coaxes the staff person toward discovering his or her own solution is a better approach.

Reflecting

Is the initial goal stated by the person being coached really the best thing to work on, or is something else more vital? A coach can only discover this by asking questions.

What Good Things Are Happening? Determining the reasons a person has to celebrate can help shed light on the direction that now needs to be taken. Asking questions specifically about what's going right helps to avoid the tendency to focus on what's going wrong.

What Should Have Priority? Not everything in a person's life is of equal importance. So what should have priority? Has the Lord been speaking about anything in particular? What is it that tends to dominate the person's thinking?

What Problems Are You Facing? Almost everyone is frustrated by something. What does the person stumble over? It's difficult to work on goals if we constantly keep hitting roadblocks that stall us or turn us aside.

What's Next? Is the person sensing a need to grow in some particular area? We can't focus on the problems forever. Sooner or later, we have to get around the roadblocks and pursue the things that are really important.

What Is Your Level of Commitment? Sometimes coaches discover that although people have worthwhile goals, they don't want to pay the price in order to do what is necessary. Ultimately, all of us have to be willing to give up, go up, and grow up. We have to give up what hinders us, go higher in our level of commitment, and grow up past adolescent attitudes if we expect to make progress.

Refocusing

Sooner or later, we come to grips with the gap between what we say we want to do and what we are actually doing. Refocusing helps us return to a sharper focus on our goals. "Most people have no idea of the giant capacity we can immediately command when we focus all of our resources on mastering a single area of our lives."[8]

But alas, it is easy to get sidetracked. The apostle Paul understood this and wrote to his friends in Corinth: "To win the contest you must deny yourselves many things that would keep you from doing your best" (1 Cor. 9:25 TLB).

Resourcing

Once we know where we want to go and have refocused our commitment to get there, we may discover that we don't have all the resources we thought we did. Often we have more than we think. People are notorious for answering the question, "What are your options?" by saying, "I don't have any. I'm stuck." We always have at least two: remain the same or change something. The same is true of resources. When we think it through, we discover we have more than we thought.

But elements may still be missing. So, by asking questions, we can help the person being coached to think of other possibilities. Who else can help? What other resources are available? How can you find what you need? Who will you ask? Where will you look?

Reviewing

From time to time, looking back over one's progress is helpful. What is going right? What did not work? What do we need to change? How can we tweak this or that? What should be done differently? What can we celebrate as a result of the progress made.

By avoiding the role of consultant (I have the answers) or counseling (Let's explore the past), but by focusing on the future, we can lead our staff, professional or volunteer, toward worthwhile goals. This will result in great personal growth for them, a sense of personal fulfillment for you, the senior pastor and coach, and value added to your church.

Build a Winning Team

Building a winning team, whether paid staff or lay volunteers, requires good coaching. Consider the acrostic FRIENDS:

- Focus on relationships
- Renew our commitment
- Invite people to participate
- Equip them to minister
- Network the body of Christ
- Demonstrate God's love
- Serve with gladness

Start Now

Late in the fourteenth century, an entomologist was checking the beams that made up the roof of the dining hall of New College, Oxford. Penknife in hand, his persistent poking revealed the beams were full of holes. Beetles were the culprits.

The problem was that some of those beams were as much as two feet square and forty-five feet long. Where could one find such beams? Someone suggested that some forested land belonging to the college might yield timber of that size.

Officials brought in the college forester to determine if he knew of any such possibilities. He said, "Well, sirs, we was wonderin' when you'd be askin'."

It seems that a hundred years earlier, when the college was built, oak trees were planted because they knew that eventually the beetles always attack the oak lumber and its disintegration was inevitable.[9]

If someone had not possessed the foresight to plant the oak trees a century earlier, they would not have been available when needed.

If we expect to have competent leaders in the future, even those who come from the ranks of our church staffs, we'd best begin to coach them now.

Action Steps

1. Examine the relationships you have with your staff members and volunteer leaders. All good coaching begins with positive relationships.
2. Choose a staff person you think would be open to a coaching relationship and propose working together to promote personal growth.
3. Evaluate your listening skills. What percentage of the time do you talk? What percentage do you listen? How can you improve the listening percentage?

9

TEAM-BUILDING

NURTURING COLLABORATIVE EFFORTS

Every leader needs a team; developing a great team that supports one another is well worth the effort.

Alone we can do so little; together we can do so much.
—HELEN KELLER

In 2002 the New England Patriots and the heavily favored St. Louis Rams met each other at Super Bowl XXXVI. As usual, announcers introduced the starting players for each team. However, New England decided to do something that no other team had ever done in a Super Bowl game. They came out as a team.

In other words, they decided not to introduce individual players. They would announce no names and would highlight no stars. The fifty-three teammates would come onto the field as a single unit. It was a striking statement that this group of well-paid professional athletes was not a group of self-seeking individuals, but a true team.

The Patriots sent a very clear message: "We're a team—we win together, we lose together." As it turned out, they won together by eking out a 20–17 victory over the Rams.[1]

Overcoming Team Dysfunctions

An athletic team does not win every time it takes the field of play. Some teams are outstanding, like the Miami Dolphins football team, who had a perfect season in 1972 and went on to win the Super Bowl. In those days, the regular season consisted of fourteen games, so after finishing 14–0, the Dolphins beat the Cleveland Browns 20–14 in the divisional playoffs. They were victorious over the Pittsburgh Steelers 21–7 for the conference championship, and then met the Washington Redskins in Super Bowl VII, winning 14–7. They are the only team in National Football League history to go undefeated in the regular season and postseason, which emphasizes how difficult it is to win every time.

Yet most of us could win more often than we do. Some teams don't win because they are dysfunctional. That was the premise of Patrick Lencioni's best-seller, *The Five Dysfunctions of a Team*. Lencioni cited five pitfalls that cause organizations to fail:

1. Absence of trust
2. Fear of conflict
3. Lack of commitment
4. Avoidance of accountability
5. Inattention to results[2]

Lack of Trust

It is next to impossible for a team to put together a winning enterprise if they don't trust each other. I once had a colleague tell me that he had grown to distrust his supervisor. He told the supervisor something in confidence and when he and the supervisor were in a group of peers, the boss pointed out my colleague and

Glue for Leaders

Warren Bennis and Burt Nanus call trust "the glue that binds followers and leaders together."

poked fun at him for being concerned about the "confidential" matter. No wonder their relationship suffered from a lack of trust.

Corrie ten Boom liked to say, "When the train goes through a tunnel and the world gets dark, do you jump out? Of course not. You sit still and trust the engineer to get you through."[3]

That's great advice if you are talking about God as the engineer to get you through life. But if you are talking about colleagues in the work place or fellow staff members in a church, you may feel like jumping off the train if your confidence is betrayed.

Fear of Conflict

Many different kinds of conflict can sidetrack a church staff.

Conflicts over Resources. Every church has a limited amount of resources. When the finance committee sets the budget, they set limitations on how much can be spent in a given area. If one staff person perceives another has received a larger budget to work with, jealousy can develop and conflict can result.

Conflicts over Influence. Nearly every staff person develops a loyal following. The person who loves the worship arts pastor may not feel so warm toward the youth pastor. In one church, the Christian education director had a warm relationship with the senior pastor. The senior pastor hired a new associate pastor and the CE director had to report to the associate. Friction developed because the CE director felt he no longer had the influence he once had with the senior pastor.

Conflicts over Personality. Let's face it, some personality types rub others the wrong way. Some people are just naturally abrasive.

Others tend to get along with everyone. Clashes will develop. It takes maturity to work through these kinds of conflicts.

Conflicts over Territories. The youth pastor wants Joe and Jane to work with him as adult youth sponsors. The worship arts pastor knows Joe and Jane have excellent voices and wants them to become involved in the upcoming church musical. Who will win? Unfortunately, unless there is mutual understanding, everyone may lose while Joe and Jane look elsewhere.

A fear of addressing these areas of conflicts will render a team dysfunctional.

Lack of Commitment

When some members of a staff feel that others aren't pulling their weight, it hurts the morale of the team. A team is only as good as its weakest member. If a member is weak, but works with all his or her heart and has unquestioned commitment, other members will be inspired by such dedication. It's when people contribute halfheartedly that other members begin to think it's all right if they work with less intensity too. Low commitment is a drag on everyone.

Avoidance of Accountability

Another stumbling block for team-building is low accountability. If no one is holding staff members accountable—and it appears some staff persons are getting away with poor performance—everybody's performance suffers. If Fred goofs off and nobody calls him to task, Susan will decide she can slack off too.

The senior pastor has to initiate regular and consistent accountability in which everyone knows the rules and plays by them, or the team's morale will drop and the quality of its performance will decline. There's a reason why John Wesley initiated class meetings to hold people accountable for their Christian walk. A staff is a small group that stimulates good performance.

Inattention to Results

Sometimes Christians get the impression that they are only responsible to be faithful. God will take care of the results. It's true that while we can plant the seed, we cannot make it grow. Only God can make it grow (1 Cor. 3:7). Nevertheless, although some seed falls by the wayside, some on rocky soil, and some on thorn-infested soil, there is also the potential that the seed that falls on good soil will bring a harvest that is hundredfold. Other seed may produce sixtyfold and still other seed thirtyfold.

Results are important, and if nobody pays attention, somebody will shirk his or her duty. The senior pastor must develop some way to measure results that takes into account faithful service and diligent effort.

The Ultimate Team-Builder

Nobody in all of Scripture is a better example of team-building than Nehemiah. He probably never would have used the term *team ministry*, but he understood the concept and used it to great advantage. In fact, the book of Nehemiah illustrates, perhaps better than any other book of the Bible, the value of teamwork.

Nehemiah held a high position in the court of King Artaxerxes. He was the cupbearer, the food taster, and in particular the wine-taster, protecting the king from poisoning. But when not engaged in those duties, he guarded the entrance to the royal apartment, and either allowed persons to enter or prevented them from entering.

Some men came from Jerusalem to Susa, where Nehemiah worked in the palace. He asked about the people in Jerusalem and how those who had survived the exile were doing.

> They said to me, "Those who survived the exile and are back in the province are in great trouble and disgrace. The wall of Jerusalem is broken down, and its gates have been burned with fire." When I heard these things, I sat down and wept. For some days I mourned and fasted and prayed before the God of heaven. Then I said: "O LORD, God of heaven, the great and awesome God, who keeps his covenant of love with those who love him and obey his commands, let your ear be attentive and your eyes open to hear the prayer your servant is praying before you day and night for your servants, the people of Israel. I confess the sins we Israelites, including myself and my father's house, have committed against you. We have acted very wickedly toward you. We have not obeyed the commands, decrees and laws you gave your servant Moses." (Neh. 1:3–7)

Team-Building Begins with a Vision

After his time of fasting and prayer, a vision began to form in Nehemiah's mind. But where does a vision begin? Don't read over that phrase too quickly, "I mourned and fasted and prayed before the God of heaven" (Neh. 1:4).

Several years ago, we used to hold evangelism and church growth conferences where we brought in the latest and greatest success stories. Pastors shared how they doubled or tripled their attendance in a relatively short period.

In essence, whether they intended it to sound this way or not, the implication was, "If you go back home and do what I did, you can have the same results."

So we would go back home and try what they tried, only to be disappointed with the results. What they failed to tell us—or perhaps we were so enamored by the success stories that we didn't hear it—was how they mourned and fasted and prayed over the lost of their city before God gave the vision that motivated them to do the things that produced their results.

In regard to team-building, once a pastor realizes the scope of the vision and begins to understand that he or she cannot achieve the vision alone, a commitment to team-building can begin to take shape.

Do you know that in some translations of the Bible, the word *saint* does not appear in the singular? And in the translations where it does appear in the singular, it is obvious that the saint is in the company of other saints. This is because we need each other. God intended for us to work together as teams.

Team-Building Expands as You Analyze the Need

Before he ever went to Jerusalem, Nehemiah began to analyze the need. He had not been there. He had not seen the wall. But in his mind, he saw it all and began to realize what he would need.

So when the king asked why he was sad, Nehemiah told him it was because the city where his fathers were buried lay in ruins and its gates had been destroyed by fire. The king asked him what he wanted. Even though Nehemiah was ready with an answer, he sent up a quick prayer. He wrote, "I prayed to the God of heaven, and I answered the king" (Neh. 2:4–5).

He had a concern for security, so he asked for letters to the governors of the provinces through which he would have to travel, thus providing safe passage until he arrived in Jerusalem. He had a concern for materials, so he asked for a letter to the keeper of the king's forest, thus giving Nehemiah the timber he would need for the gates. The king gave Nehemiah more than he asked for and even provided army officers and cavalry to escort him along the way.

Once he arrived in Jerusalem, Nehemiah lost very little time. He set out at night with a few men and began to inspect the wall. As soon as it was feasible, he gathered the city leaders and began to share his vision, give his testimony about the king's help, and something of his analysis of the problem. Then he challenged them: "Let us rebuild the wall of Jerusalem, and we will no longer be in disgrace" (2:17).

As you begin to analyze the need, it will occur to you that you must have help. Then you will begin, as Nehemiah did, to recruit the partners you need to be effective in your ministry. Whether you add paid staff or recruit and train volunteers, once you have the vision and analyze the need, you will begin to choose your team.

Team-Building Compounds as You Choose Your Team Members

The people you choose to serve with you on your team make all the difference in the world. Choose the right people and your result will be terrific. Choose people who "play well with others." You will train them to follow your leadership, but finding people who already have a positive attitude will help tremendously.

Benefits of Developing Leaders

There are several benefits of developing spiritual leaders. These things are true whether talking about paid staff or volunteers:

1. You encourage a deeper spiritual walk.
2. You enjoy a wider sphere of influence.
3. You set higher expectations for leaders.
4. You produce longer tenures for pastors and people.

I read about a farmer who used to hitch up his old mule to a two-horse plow every day and say, "Get up, Beauregard. Get up, Satchel. Get up, Robert. Get up, Betty Lou."

One day his neighbor overheard this routine and asked the farmer, "How many names does that mule have?"

"Oh, he only has one," answered the farmer. "His name is Pete. But I put blinders on him and call out all the other names so he will think other mules are working with him. He has a better attitude when he's part of a team."

We all do better when we're part of a team.

Effective Team-Building

Every situation is different. But a few basic ideas can help you build your team more effectively.

Communication Is Key

Some teams never become fully developed—and certainly never achieve their potential—simply because people aren't on the same page. Communication is the key.

Laying out the facts of what your team is trying to accomplish is important. It may seem as if you are stating the obvious. But stating the obvious is not always a bad thing. The world is full of people who see the problems; they could state the obvious too. Yet they haven't done anything about it. The world is full of people who have dreamed great dreams and have had great ideas. But the world takes its hat off and applauds people who figure out how to make the dreams come true and translate the great ideas into concrete accomplishments.

So what challenge is your team facing? Does everyone know what the challenge is? We hear about bills in Congress that are hundreds of pages and thousands of words, and you wonder if anyone ever reads the measures for which they are voting. How delightful when a leader defines a challenge in a few words that everyone can understand.

In the process of rallying the troops, be sure you are motivating, not manipulating. The difference? Is it good for your kingdom or is it best for God's kingdom? Is it self-serving or are you serving others? You may want to pull together some trusted advisors who can help you think it through and be sure you are doing what is in the best interest of the kingdom. All of us can fool ourselves at times. There is safety in godly collaboration and counsel.

Focus Is Essential

Pat Summitt recently retired as the coach of the Lady Volunteers basketball team at the University of Tennessee. She coached them for more than thirty-five years. She and her teams won eight national championships and never had a losing season. She knows very well that games don't always go according to the best-laid plans. She says that in the high pressure of a forty-minute basketball game, "You have to learn quickly from your mistakes and to change your approach accordingly. Basketball is very much about momentum, and if things are going badly, you need to change that momentum with a timeout."

During the timeout, she only has ninety seconds to make the changes needed. Imagine having only ninety seconds to analyze, interpret, make a decision, and communicate that decision to your players.

How does she do it? She says, "I have to focus not on myself or on what I'm feeling, but on what my team is feeling. So, as a coach, I try to empty myself of my own emotions, and I try to convey—through words, tone and body language—what my players need to hear."[4]

That one phrase—"I try to empty myself"—sounds almost like a spiritual concept. If she is willing to go into a self-emptying mode for the sake of a basketball game, how much more do we need to do whatever is necessary to stay focused on the objective in the work God has called us to do? For the sake of your team-building, stay focused.

Establishing Your Identity Is Crucial

A colleague told me about a friend of his, a Canadian, who was traveling by train in England. On the trains in Great Britain, you can walk up to the first class section and if seats are available, you can be seated. When the conductor comes by and looks at your ticket, if he sees you have a coach ticket but are sitting in first class, you can simply pay the difference and keep your seat in first class.

This is what happened to the Canadian. The conductor looked at his ticket and told him how much he owed. The Canadian did what many people do when traveling in foreign countries. He pulled some money out of is pocket, laid it on the table, and said, "Take whatever you need."

The conductor said, "Are you from the United States?"

"No, from Canada."

"Same thing."

Indignant, but unabashed, the Canadian asked, "Are you Irish?"

The conductor quickly said, "No, I'm English."

"Same thing."

The conductor walked away, muttering words that he did not learn in Sunday school.

We know, of course, that American and Canadian, Irish and English are not the same things. All of us are protective of our identity. We know who we are and it is important to us.

Have you established an identity for your team? Is there a certain amount of legitimate pride in who you are and what you stand for? Have you developed some practices as a team, some things you do and some things you don't do, because you are part of the team?

When Victor Seribriakoff was fifteen, his teacher told him he would never finish school and that he should drop out and learn a trade. Victor took the advice and for the next seventeen years he was an itinerant, doing a variety of odd jobs. Since people told him he was a dunce, for seventeen years he acted like a dunce. At the age of thirty-two, an amazing transformation occurred. An evaluation revealed that he was a genius with an IQ of 161.

Consequently, he started acting like a genius. Since that time, he has written books, secured a number of patents, and has become a successful businessman. This former dropout was elected as chair of the International Mensa Society, which has only one membership qualification—you must have an IQ of at least 140.[5]

Did he suddenly become smart at age thirty-two? No. What changed was the way he saw himself. And the way your team looks at itself will affect its performance too. Build some legitimate pride in who you are as a team. Establish and maintain your identity.

Every leader must have a team. As I said before, you can't do it alone. No one can. Every leader must be surrounded by a team.

Finding Your Team Members

A colleague told me about his frustration at a church he pastored. The church needed workers for the various ministries of the church, and it seemed as if all the new people who came through the doors carried baggage with them. He would often think, "With so many problems of their own, how will they ever be ready to minister to others?"

Scarred Helpers

One day a handsome young couple showed up for worship. She was cute as a button; he was handsome; they were well-dressed; they were already Christians; and they both had experience working as laypeople in a church. They appeared to be any pastor's answer for a new couple to jump in and help with ministry.

It wasn't long, however, before he discovered they could not stand each other. Their marriage was a mess. Once again, the pastor plunged into the Slough of Despond, like Christian in *Pilgrim's Progress*.

Of course, as the pastor thought about it, he was wise enough to know that his expectations were unrealistic. What is the church for if not to reach the lost, least, last, hurting, and broken?

Use People's Gifts

I encourage pastors to find out their laypersons' spiritual gifts. Teach them how to use their gifts to maximum advantage. Give them information, insight, inspiration, and some new skills that will make them more effective. From leading ministry teams to serving in the community, from welcoming newcomers to calling on shut-ins, lay leaders who are equipped for ministry will multiply your impact immeasurably.

Then, by the grace of God, we help them come to terms with their weaknesses and receive grace from God so they can be a blessing to others.

Getting the Right People in the Right Places

Ted Engstrom was president of World Vision International and was known worldwide for his management expertise. Someone asked him, "What is the bottom line on building a strong team?" You might expect a fairly long, complicated, perhaps even hard-to-understand answer. Instead his profound response was, "Getting round pegs in round holes."[6]

Sometimes pastors—especially solo pastors who cannot afford to hire staff and must depend on volunteers—feel that because we don't have the best-qualified people, we are required to force any peg into any available hole just to get the job filled. Over time, we learn what people's spiritual gifts are and how we can best help them work in the area of their strength.

A Positive Attitude

A positive attitude is like the oil in an engine. It is a lubricant that enables the mind's creation, solution-oriented power to respond to your command. A negative attitude drains the mind of this essential lubricant, freezing and shutting it down. A positive attitude sees a problem as an opportunity, a difficulty as a challenge. A negative attitude does the opposite and is the prescription for defeat.

—David McNally

People Who Are Consistent

Cal Ripken Jr. made a name for himself by showing up consistently, day after day, for 2,632 consecutive games over a period of seventeen seasons. As admirable as that is, he took some criticism, particularly when he experienced a batting slump.

On one occasion, *Sports Illustrated* did an article on him and talked about his "somber solitude." Ripken says he was not in somber solitude, but the piece did get his attention, and he was concerned about his hitting.

For a time, he even considered sitting out a game. If he took a day off, it would end his consecutive streak of showing up every day, but it might end his batting slump. It might take off the pressure. Maybe if he sat out a game, that would do it.[7]

But he did not give in to that thinking. He continued playing and became the poster child for consistency.

We all appreciate people who show up and do their job week after week, regardless of the circumstances. They will serve if they get recognition; they will serve if they don't. It's not about recognition. It's about being part of the team and serving for Jesus' sake.

No Room for Prima Donnas

I read somewhere about a rehearsal at the Metropolitan Opera House in New York. The musical maestro, Arturo Toscanini, offered some constructive criticism to a featured soloist. The singer, however, was too proud to accept his help and expressed her resentment by exclaiming, "You cannot treat me like this! I am a star!"

Toscanini looked at the other members of the cast, the orchestra, the chorus, the technical crew, and responded, "Madame, there are only stars in the heavens. There are no stars in my performances!"[8]

It's the same in church. We're in this together, all on the same team, striving to accomplish God's purpose for our church and community.

Start Now

Unlike the Miami Dolphins who turned in a perfect season in 1972, many athletes are unable to compete at that level. But they are still athletes.

I love the story of the girl who waited at the starting line, anticipating the firing of the gun that would launch the runners forward in her event at the Special Olympics. The split-second she heard the gun, she yelled, "I'm gone!" And she was—not with what most people would call Olympic-form, however. Hitting every lane, she propelled herself around the track forty yards ahead of everyone else.

When she reached the finish line, she stopped. Instead of crossing, she turned around and waited for her friends to catch up. When all six runners arrived, they held hands and crossed the finish line together, as she shouted, "We all win!" What a great spirit to describe what we do in the church!

Now, don't misunderstand. We need the best qualified, the sharpest, the most competent people we can get to form our teams for ministry. But at the end of the day it's not a competition. It's a cooperation!

Action Steps

1. How are your team members held accountable? Do they understand the expectations? What do you need to change for the better?
2. How does your team handle conflict? What kind of venue do you have for people to agreeably disagree?
3. Evaluate your team's identity. What can you change to improve the way your team sees itself?

10

AFFIRMATION
GIVING APPROPRIATE RECOGNITION

While staff persons need varying amounts of affirmation, everybody needs recognition now and then.

Compliments by their very nature are highly biodegradable and tend to dissolve hours or days after we receive them—which is why we can always use another.
—PHYLLIS THEROUX

Dr. Jo Anne Lyon tells about her son Mark coming home from kindergarten and handing her his report card. She didn't bother to get down on his eye level. Rather, she pulled the card from the envelope and read it from her five-foot-seven viewpoint. Of the twenty-plus items on the card, the teacher had noted two or three areas for improvement. Instantly, she looked down on Mark and began to tell him what he needed to do to improve.

His eyes clouded with disappointment as he looked up and said, "Can't I do anything right?" As pain stabbed her heart, she fell to the couch and pulled him into her arms. They went through the report card, item by item. She emphasized the affirmations, after which the areas that needed improvement were reachable and manageable.[1]

Other adults are notorious for doing just what Dr. Lyon did—jumping on the negatives before remembering to emphasize the positives. As we grow up, we have no less need for affirmation.

However, we often simply learn not to expect it. Instead we often live in fear of someone pointing out the negatives rather than affirming us.

When We Fail to Praise

Benjamin Franklin had an interesting theory about the origin of "censure and backbiting." He carried on a considerable correspondence with Jared Eliot, a friend who happened to be an expert on scientific agriculture as well as pastor of a Congregational church. In one letter, Franklin wrote that the world would be better off if people were allowed to praise themselves instead of pretending to be indifferent to praise.

He observed that children praised themselves. They said things like, "I am a good boy; am I not a good girl?" But adults corrected them, so the children quit saying such things. Franklin said he thought this led them to begin to censure others, "which is only a roundabout way of praising themselves." It is like saying, "I am such an honest person or wise or good that I could never indulge in such behavior." Franklin said, "I wish men had not been taught to dam up natural currents, to the overflowing and damage of their neighbor's grounds."[2]

The Absence of Parental Approval

Many people grow up seeking the praise and affirmation of their parents. Lee Strobel tells about how he hungered to hear his father say, "Lee, I'm proud of you. You're really special to me. Son, I really like who you are."

Looking back, Strobel says his father was probably trying to communicate such feelings in other ways, but it would have meant so much to *hear* it. He is sure his workaholism through the years was an effort to heal the wound created by the lack of affirmation and an effort to earn his father's respect.

His father died while Lee was in law school. He flew back home for the wake and was amazed at the people who stopped by to greet him and said such things as: "Are you Wally's son? Oh, he was so proud of you. . . . When you went off to Yale Law School, he was just thrilled. When you'd have a byline in the *Tribune*, he was always showing it to everybody. He couldn't stop talking about you! You were such an important part of his life."[3]

Yet his father had not told him these things. He had to wait until his father was dead to learn them. How would it have changed his life had he known these things when his father was alive?

It is easy to take such things for granted. Likewise, it is easy to ignore people we should recognize, overlook people we should notice, or slight people we should affirm.

Taking People for Granted

Former Speaker of the House Tip O'Neill told about a woman he took for granted. On one election day, an elderly neighbor stopped him after she left the polls. She said, "Tip, I voted for you today, even though you didn't ask me."

He said, "Mrs. O'Brien, I've known you all my life. I took your garbage out for you, mowed your lawn, shoveled snow for you. I didn't think I had to ask."

In a motherly tone she said, "Tip, it's always *nice* to be asked."[4]

Only a Servant?

Sometimes managers and leaders, including senior pastors, think about their employees simply as servants who are supposed to do what they are paid to do. Maybe they remember the passage of Scripture in which Jesus referred to a servant who came in from the field. The master did not tell the servant to sit down and eat, but rather to prepare the master's supper. The master would not thank the servant, but would rather expect obedience.

Jesus made the point that we are God's servants. He said, "So you also, when you have done everything you were told to do, should say, 'We are unworthy servants; we have only done our duty'" (Luke 17:10).

This is not justification for treating staff persons, even though they are employed, like servants. All of us are indebted to God for forgiveness, for the promise of eternal life, even for life itself. Nevertheless, even God gives us a picture of a future time when he will say, "Well done, good and faithful servant! You have been faithful with a few things; I will put you in charge of many things. Come and share your master's happiness!" (Matt. 25:21).

A Servant of Servants

Let every day, therefore, be a day of humility; condescend to all the weaknesses and infirmities of your fellow-creatures, cover their frailties, love their excellencies, encourage their virtues, relieve their wants, rejoice in their prosperities, compassionate their distress, receive their friendship, overlook their unkindness, forgive their malice, be a servant of servants, and condescend to do the lowest offices to the lowest of mankind.

—William Law

In fact, if we fail to affirm our people, whether paid staff or unpaid volunteers, they will soon become unwilling workers.

William J. Schwarz gives an insightful warning: “If the structure or systems of the organization cause people to feel unvalued, unworthy, or unwise, they will look for ways to beat the system.”[5]

The Value of Affirmation

The apostle Paul understood the value of giving affirmation. He also recognized that not everyone is alike. When giving final instructions in one letter, he wrote, “Warn those who are idle, encourage the timid, help the weak, be patient with everyone” (1 Thess. 5:14). Parents know that even children reared in the same household respond differently to various stimuli. A sharp word can nearly crush the spirit of some children, while more stern punishment does little to dissuade others.

So, while using different strokes for different folks, we understand that everybody can use some kind of affirmation. The Bible gives a variety of ways to affirm people.

Listen

I have spoken about listening in a couple of earlier chapters of this book, but I must return to it here. James said, “My dear brothers, take note of this: Everyone should be quick to listen, slow to speak and slow to become angry” (James 1:19). Without saying a word, just the act of listening affirms people. It tacitly says, “I respect you. What you have to say is important to me. You have my full attention.” It is an unspoken affirmation.

However, only pretending to listen, or doing something else while a person is talking to you, implies that what they say is not important to you. It does not take a big leap of imagination for your staff member to assume that he or she is not important to you if you don't take the time to listen.

Empathize

"Rejoice with those who rejoice," wrote Paul. "Mourn with those who mourn" (Rom. 12:15). It is often easier to mourn with those who are suffering some kind of loss than it is to rejoice with those who rejoice.

If your youth pastor has completed a successful retreat at which several young people committed their lives to Christ, rejoice with him or her. If your worship arts pastor has directed an outstanding holiday musical attended by a record number of persons, why not celebrate? Their success is your success. If you don't honestly feel that way, spend some time on your knees until you can rejoice with them.

Showing concern when they have suffered loss is equally important, but often easier to do because we tend to be caregivers. Be an affirming person. Leil Lowndes observes, "There are two kinds of people in this life. Those who walk into a room and say, 'Well, here I am.' And those who walk in and say, 'Ahh, there you are.' Let us each strive to be an 'Ahh, there you are' person."[6] What a great way to affirm others, by mourning when it is needed and rejoicing when it is appropriate.

Comfort

Paul said, "Praise be to the God and Father of our Lord Jesus Christ, the Father of compassion and the God of all comfort, who comforts us in all our troubles, so that we can comfort those in any trouble with the comfort we ourselves have received from God" (2 Cor. 1:3–4).

Fred Smith made a distinction between sympathy and comfort, declaring they are two different things. "I don't mind spending time comforting someone, but I won't spend time sympathizing. Sympathy is an addictive emotion; people want more and more and more. Comfort, on the other hand, brings a light to the darkness. Comfort produces progress; sympathy doesn't."[7]

However you define it, be known as a person who gives comfort. Be sure your staff is not exempt from receiving comfort if they need it. As the senior pastor, your comfort is not just for parishioners going through difficult times. It is for your staff as well. They feel deeply affirmed when you provide comfort.

Carry Burdens

Paul wrote, "Carry each other's burdens, and in this way you will fulfill the law of Christ" (Gal. 6:2). Later he talked about each person carrying his own load (Gal. 6:5). Greek scholars tell us that the word for "load" refers to something like a soldier's pack. It is a load that one person can certainly carry without assistance. Life piles some burdens on us, however, that would force us to the ground without someone—or perhaps several someones—coming alongside to help us carry them.

What a great affirmation when you come alongside staff persons, holding them accountable for what they are capable of carrying themselves, but supporting and encouraging them when the load becomes too heavy.

Encourage

After assuring the Thessalonians that the Lord was going to return and that eventually we would live forever with him, Paul said, "Therefore encourage one another and build each other up, just as in fact you are doing" (1 Thess. 5:11).

Forced to quit school when he was only twelve years old because of his father's imprisonment, Charles got a job in a rat-infested workplace. He wanted to be a writer and worked at it in his spare time. But his efforts were rejected time after time. One day he received yet another rejection letter, but this one was a little different. The editor said he should continue writing because the world needed him. That provided sufficient encouragement to keep him going until Charles Dickens produced such masterpieces as *Oliver Twist*, *A Tale of Two Cities*, and *A Christmas Carol*.[8]

You never know what your words of encouragement may mean to someone struggling to succeed. Be an encourager. It's a strong way to affirm others.

Show Kindness

"Always try to be kind to each other," Paul wrote (1 Thess. 5:15). What could possibly prevent people from being kind to others? Being too busy. Not paying attention. Breezing through life with blinders on. All those things can prevent you from being kind.

But if you are paying attention, treating others with respect, smiling often, treating people with gentleness, you will become known as a person of kindness. As Leo Buscaglia said, "Too often we underestimate the power of a touch, a smile, a kind word, a listening ear, an honest compliment, or the smallest act of caring, all of which have the potential to turn a life around."[9]

The Continuum of Affirmation

People have varying needs for affirmation. On the Continuum of Affirmation chart (below), you will note that some people come across as being extremely dependent. They are almost desperate for affirmation. On the other extreme are those who are independent. They don't need it and, in fact, are skeptical when it appears.

Between those two extremes are the multitude of our coworkers, staff members, and volunteers. They don't require a pat on the back every day, or a word of encouragement upon every meeting. Yet neither are they like the proverbial camel who can cross the desert of employment without even a thimbleful of affirmation.

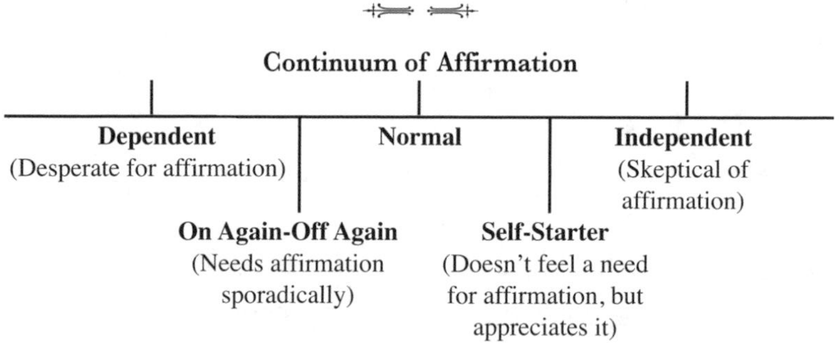

Dependent

In the course of your ministry, you will meet people who have so little self-confidence, they will cling to every word of encouragement like a snapping turtle that refuses to let go of a stick. If you happen to be the kind of person who finds it easy to give compliments, these low-confidence people will beat a path to your door. They thrive on positive attention.

We have all heard the stories of those who grew up with no self-confidence. Walt Disney was told he had no talent. Long before there was a Walmart, F. W. Woolworth built a "five-and-ten-cent store" concept into a nationwide chain of stores. But Woolworth was told early on that he had no business or social skills. Both Thomas Edison and Albert Einstein were labeled as "slow learners" and their teachers suggested they drop out of school.

There are still people who believe the negative talk they've been told. They crave any encouragement you may give. Staff members with such low self-confidence will perform better if they know you believe in them.

On Again-Off Again

Others are not quite so low on the self-confidence ladder, but they are easily discouraged. Some days they can conquer the world; the next day they want to crawl in a hole. We all need someone to believe in us and these people will demonstrate that need with a fair degree of regularity.

They prove the truth of Elbert Hubbard's statement: "If we do well, we want our work commended, our faith corroborated. The individual who thinks well of you, who keeps his mind on your good qualities, and does not look for your flaws, is your friend. Who is my brother? I'll tell you: he is the one who recognizes the good in me."[10]

Normal

"Normal" may be a misnomer. It's fairly difficult to define. In fact, some have concluded, with Patsy Clairmont, that "normal is just a setting on your dryer."[11] As I am using it, normal is that middle ground, however thinly populated, midway between dependent and independent on the affirmation continuum. It's those "average" people for whom affirmation is important, but not all-important. They welcome affirmation, but don't actively seek it.

The problem with normal, however, is pinning it down. Some people may equate normal with ideal. So they think of a normal family as a "Leave it to Beaver" family, with June Cleaver always at home when "The Beave" walks through the door. Or they think of an "Ozzie and Harriet Nelson" kind of family, where even Dad always seems to be at home or has wisdom for every situation.

The problem with those families is that they don't exist, except on television in the 1950s and 1960s. John Bradshaw believes at least 98 percent of us come from dysfunctional families. In other words, we come from families that are "out of balance and often teeter on the edge of crisis."[12]

We could argue about percentages. I don't want to think the number of dysfunctional families is that high. Yet many people come from backgrounds where they received little or no positive feedback. This situation is likely to produce a preponderance of people on the left side of the affirmation continuum, greatly in need of encouragement. Thus, the problem of defining what is normal.

Affirm Them

Your volunteers need your affirmation. Affirming your worship team is just one example of this need. Your team may hear criticism more often than they hear praise. So take every opportunity to affirm them. Let them know what a crucial part they play in leading the congregation in worship.

Let's just say normal is the point at which people move from one side of the continuum to the other.

Self-Starter

Some fortunate people—or perhaps "disciplined" is a better word—are self-starters. They don't need encouragement or instructions to know what to do or to get started doing it. These are the people who don't wait for a pat on the back to begin heading toward their goals. However, while they may not feel a need for affirmation, they appreciate it when it comes their way.

As Ken Blanchard and Spencer Johnson observed, "The key to developing people is to catch them doing something right."[13] To such people, a word of encouragement provides stimulation that propels them into greater accomplishment. They're going to do their job anyway. But your coming along at the right time with the right word of affirmation gives them extra incentive. They will work that much harder because they are grateful for your acceptance.

Independent

A few hard-working people reside at the extreme right-hand end of the affirmation continuum. They're like the Energizer Bunny who work hard, and are "so strong and so busy that any attempts at praising them would be nothing more than a pesky gnat flying around one's face. They would brush it off with a look of confusion." They may even "view attempts at praise with great suspicion."[14]

Even so, make affirmation a way of life. It will encourage and stimulate the fainthearted. Although it may confuse those who are highly motivated, it will have a cumulatively positive effect over time.

Practical Ways to Affirm

There are many ways to affirm people.

Phone Calls

With cell phones today, we can reach people almost anytime, anywhere. While you will want to be considerate of their time and schedule, calling or texting with a sincere compliment at an appropriate time, or even a surprising time, will mean a great deal.

Personal Notes

A hand-written note has become almost a relic of antiquity. Think of how much we know about some historical figures because of the correspondence they kept up with friends near and far. Will some future historian remain frustrated because the majority of our correspondence disappeared with the click of the "delete" key?

At any rate, a hand-written note carries a great deal of weight. My handwriting is not always legible, but even if people don't know precisely what I have written, they know it's a positive affirmation because it came from me. Short notes make a lasting impression.

It does not have to be around a holiday or even about a specific event. Just a note saying, "I appreciate your great attitude about working here. Thanks!" will be meaningful.

A colleague told me about sending a note of appreciation to a retired mentor, a man who had influenced his life decades earlier. A few weeks later,

The Power of a Note

We wildly underestimate the power of the tiniest personal touch. And of all personal touches, I find the short, handwritten "nice job" note to have the highest impact. (It even seems to beat a call—something about the tangibility.)

he heard back from his old friend. He said, "You'll never know how much your note meant. I had fallen earlier and wrenched my shoulder. It laid me up for awhile, and I was feeling pretty useless when your note came. Thanks so much."

Only God can orchestrate timing like that. Your note may come at just the time a person needs it most.

Personal Visit

I wrote in a previous chapter, "Manage by walking around." Getting out of your office and walking to a colleague's office or cubicle to say, "Hey, I noticed what you did the other day, and I wanted you to know how much it meant to me. Great job!" will speak volumes. In fact, it probably has a greater impact than a note, a phone call, or inviting him or her to come to your office to compliment them.

Public Expressions

When you acknowledge someone in front of an audience, you potentially make scores, hundreds, thousands of people happy, depending on the size of your church.

It also sets a great example. It gives others an opportunity to express their appreciation to the same person, multiplying the effect.

Newsletters

Whether published on paper or published online, a newsletter provides another opportunity to give well-deserved kudos. At the end of a campaign, following a season of hard work, after a team has performed particularly well, or after the holidays when your staff is exhausted from the extra work, it's an excellent time to say, "Thanks, well done!"

Dinners

A colleague told me about a tradition at his church where he had two assistant pastors. The entire staff, along with administrative assistants and secretaries, went out for lunch whenever anyone had a birthday. The birthday person did not have to pay. They usually gave just cards, no elaborate gifts. But it was a way of saying, "You are important to us. We celebrate your special day, your friendship, and we value you as a colleague in the ministry."

One colleague who had a rather large staff had quarterly birthday lunches, honoring those who had birthdays within a certain timeframe. He said these celebrations improved morale and enhanced team spirit.

Special dinners honoring staff persons around holidays can also provide a way to affirm people and emphasize their value to the team.

The Whisper Test

Mary Ann Bird has told about growing up, knowing she was different. Born with a cleft palate, she understood early on from the comments of her classmates in elementary school that they saw her as different.

When people asked what happened to her lip, she would tell them she had fallen as a baby and cut it on a piece of glass. She was convinced that no one outside her family ever loved her or even liked her. Until she entered Mrs. Leonard's second grade class.

Mary Ann could not hear well out of one ear, but she did not want to add that to her list of deficiencies, so she learned to cheat on hearing tests. The teacher would conduct a "whisper test," whereby each child would go to the door of the classroom, turn sideways, close one ear with a finger, and the teacher would whisper something from her desk, which the child would repeat. This was done for each ear.

Mary Ann discovered that no one checked to see how tightly each ear was blocked, so she pretended to block her good ear.

When her turn came, the classroom was empty except for her and her teacher. She pretended to block her ear and then Mrs. Leonard spoke the words that changed Mary Ann's life forever: "I wish you were my little girl."[15]

Many staff persons would never verbalize it, but they are waiting for similar words that assure them they are worthwhile persons, appreciated as individuals, and valuable to the team. By the way, there's no need to whisper it. Say it clearly, with confidence and sincerity.

Action Steps

1. Evaluate your staff relationships. How long has it been since you gave a sincere compliment to each person? What can you do to improve your own performance?
2. As you think about your staff, where does each person fit on the affirmation continuum? How has your record of affirmation confirmed that you understand where they each fit?
3. Think about your interactions with staff in the past six months. How have you done at listening? Empathizing? Comforting? Encouraging? Showing kindness?

APPENDIX

Chapter 2: Form for Reference Checking

(Can help determine if a potential staff member is a good fit for the culture of your church.)

Candidate: ____

Reference's Name: ______________________________________

Phone: ____

Date/Time Called: ______________________________________

1. Hello, ________. My name is ________. I am the (senior pastor or search committee member). (Candidate) is being considered for a possible pastoral position in our church and gave your name as a personal reference. I'd like to verify a few facts with you. Would this be a convenient time to spend fifteen or twenty minutes visiting with me about (candidate)? (If not, is there a time we could schedule that would be more convenient for you?)
2. The position for which (candidate) is being considered involves serving as the (type of pastor—solo, senior, assistant, etc.) pastor of a church averaging (number) persons in its main worship service. It is located in (type of community) and will require a pastor who has special skills in (list examples).
3. What personal or professional relationship have you had with (candidate)?
4. What are some qualities about (candidate) that you appreciate or admire?

5. What are your observations about (candidate's) work habits or style compared to other pastors you might know?
6. (Reference), I'm sure you understand the tremendous pressure pastoral work involves. The pastor of the church (candidate) is being considered for will have to work well with a wide variety of personalities, be able to cope well with conflicts, encourage individuals in their personal and spiritual growth, provide vision and leadership for the future, model godly character, possess good preaching skills, and be able to gain cooperation from others for ministry (or list other qualities you are seeking in this person). While we both know there is no such thing as the perfect pastor, all of us have weaknesses that counterbalance most of our strengths. I am interested in knowing some of the areas in which you think (candidate) might need further development or improvement.
7. How would you evaluate (candidate's) spiritual vitality? Can you give me an example or a specific instance that impressed you positively or negatively in this area?
8. How effective has (candidate) been at winning people to Christ and getting them involved in the church? Do you know anyone personally whom he/she has won to Christ and the church?
9. What can you tell me about (candidate's) management style? How does he/she handle things like attention to detail, delegating work to others, building and leading teams, helping others develop vision or goals, or dealing with crisis situations?
10. Some people need lots of ideas and direction from others; some work well if you give them a clear list of job expectations and

only a moderate amount of supervision; some work best if you give them an assignment and then leave them alone to be creative; some always seem to have their own plans and priorities and do not welcome advice or input from others. In your judgment, what is the best management style to use with (candidate)?

11. Based on what you know about (candidate's) track record and relationships, how well do you think he/she would do in a church like the one I described to you earlier? In what areas do you think he/she might experience difficulties? Is there another setting in which you think he/she might do better?
12. If given the opportunity, would you want (candidate) to be your pastor? Why or why not?
13. Are you aware of any circumstances, attitudes, or problems that wave a caution flag about (candidate) being considered for a ministry leadership position?
14. Before we go, is there a question you wish I had asked you?
15. Thank you for your time and help.

Chapter 4: Strategy Worksheet

Ask staff members to complete this worksheet for all major projects assigned to them. It will help them turn the priority into a reality.

Project____

Leader____

Date____

Needs: What specific needs is this project designed to meet and for whom?

1.
2.
3.
4.
5.

Purpose: Why are we tackling this project?

Roadblocks: What are the biggest challenges to completing the project?

1.
2.
3.

Resources: What key resources we will bring to bear?

1.
2.
3.

Goals: What specific, measurable results are we trying to achieve?

1.
2.
3.

— adapted from Bobb Biehl, *Dream Energy* (2001, Quick Wisdom Publishing), 186.

Chapter 5: Ministry Reviews of Objectives and Goals

Purpose: *To encourage and affirm each staff person and establish more effective communication between staff and church leadership, and to design clear, realistic goals and objectives for the upcoming year. This form is to be filled out by the one being reviewed: (Name)*

Part I – Job Description

Include your Job Description as the next page in this document.

Read through the Job Description and make any comments or suggested changes, as desired.

Part II – Goals and Objectives of the Past Year

For _________ _________ through _________ _________

(month) (year) (month) (year)

Significant Accomplishments (List major projects completed from the past year)

1.
2.
3.

Ongoing Responsibilities (Describe progress achieved in past year)

1.
2.
3.

Opportunites for Growth and Development (List areas where you see room for improvement)

1.
2.
3.

Part III – Goals and Objectives of the Coming Year

For ________ ________ through ________ ________
(month) (year) (month) (year)

New Goals and Objectives (New initiatives for the following year)

Progress: _______ (Review Date)

1.
2.
3.

Ongoing Responsibilities (Renewed initiatives from a previous year)

1.
2.
3.

Professional Development or Outside Ministry (Further educational or additional ministry opportunities)

1.
2.
3.

—adapted from http://www.buildingchurchleaders.com/downloads/bestchurchpractices/staffevaluations/bp02-b.html, accessed 10/30/11.

Chapter 8: Powerful Coaching Questions

Relate (establish coaching relationship and agenda)

1. How are you doing?
2. Where are you now?
3. How can I be praying for you?
4. What do you want to address?
5. How can we work together?

Reflect (discover and explore key issues)

1. What can we celebrate?
2. What's really important?
3. What obstacles are you facing?
4. Where do you want to go?
5. How committed are you?

Refocus (plan priorities and action steps)

1. What do you want to accomplish?
2. What are possible ways to get there?
3. Which path will you choose?
4. What will you do (who, what, when, where, how?)
5. How will you measure your progress?

Resource (provide support and encouragement)

1. What resources will you need to accomplish your goals (people, finances, knowledge, etc.)?
2. What resources do you already have?
3. What resources are you missing?
4. Where will you find the resources you need?
5. What can I do to support you?

Review (evaluate, celebrate, and revise plans)

1. What's working (wins since our last conversation)?
2. What's not working?

3. What are you learning ("ah-has")?
4. What needs to change?
5. What else needs to be done?
6. What further training would be helpful?
7. What's next in our coaching relationship?

—*Coaching 101: Discover the Power of Coaching* by Robert Logan and Sherilyn Carlton (2003, ChurchSmart), 119–120.

NOTES

Chapter 1

1. Gordon MacDonald, *The Life God Blesses: Weathering the Storms of Life That Threaten the Soul* (Nashville: Thomas Nelson, 1994), 1–4.
2. "Who Said That About—Character?" *New Man*, January/February 1997, 18.
3. "Peter I," accessed August 30, 2011, http://www.answers.com/topic/peter-the-great.
4. "To a Louse," accessed September 1, 2011, http://www.worldburnsclub.com/poems/translations/552.htm.
5. Clark Cothern, "A Long Train of Thought," accessed March 1, 2012, http://www.christianitytoday.com/le/1998/winter/8l1071.html.
6. MacDonald, 141.
7. Ibid., 183.
8. Chris Cree, "Seven Ways to Start Leading Yourself," accessed June 12, 2011, http://successcreeations.com/23/7-ways-to-start-leading-yourself/.
9. David McCullough, *Mornings on Horseback: The Story of an Extraordinary Family, a Vanished Way of Life and the Unique Child Who Became Theodore Roosevelt* (New York: Simon and Schuster, 2001), 338.
10. John C. Maxwell, *Developing the Leaders Around You: How to Help Others Reach Their Full Potential* (Nashville: Thomas Nelson, 1995), 104.
11. "Samuel Taylor Coleridge," accessed September 10, 2011, http://www.brainyquote.com/quotes/quotes/s/samueltayl108501.html.
12. Peggy Noonan, *When Character was King: A Story of Ronald Reagan* (New York: Viking, 2001), 82–83.
13. Brian Tracy, "Positive Attitude," accessed September 10, 2011, http://www.motivatingquotes.com/briantracy.htm.
14. "Phillips Brooks," accessed September 10, 2011, http://www.quotationspage.com/quote/2815.html.

15. "Theodore Roosevelt," accessed September 10, 2011, http://www.livinglifefully.com/character.html.
16. "Dwight L. Moody," accessed September 10, 2011, http://www.jesus-is-savior.com/Great%20Men%20of%20God/dwight_moody-quotes.htm.
17. "Stephen Covey," accessed September 10, 2011, http://www.great-inspirational-quotes.com/habit-quotes.html.
18. J. R. Miller, cited in John C. Maxwell, *The 21 Irrefutable Laws of Leadership: Follow Them and People Will Follow You* (Nashville: Thomas Nelson, 1998), 62.

Chapter 2

1. David L. McKenna, *Power to Follow, Grace to Lead: Strategy for the Future of Christian Leadership* (Dallas, Tex.: Word Publishing, 1989), 44.
2. Cited in Chris W. Tornquist, "Reading Between the Lines: The Problem of Unwritten Expectations," *Christian Education Journal,* Volume X, Number 2 (Winter 1990): 18.
3. The quotation has also been attributed to P. T. Barnum, Mark Twain, and the poet John Lydgate. Accessed September 14, 2011, http://wiki.an- swers,com/Who_said_'You_can_fool_all_the_people_some_of_the_time_and_some_of_the_people_all_the_time_but_you_cannot_fool_all_the_people_all_the_time'.
4. Richard P. Hansen, "The Sound of Clashing Expectations," *Leadership* (Summer 1984): 79.
5. James A. Davey and Warren Bird, "They Like Me, They Like Me Not," *Leadership* (Summer 1984): 77.

Chapter 3

1. "Clouded Vision," *Leadership* (Winter 1984): 76.
2. Ibid.
3. Ibid.
4. Cited by John Maxwell in *Failing Forward: Turning Mistakes into Stepping Stones for Success* (Nashville: Thomas Nelson, 2000), 155.
5. Ibid.
6. Fred Smith, *Learning to Lead: Bringing Out the Best in People*, vol. 5, *The Leadership Library* (Waco, Tex.: Word, 1986), 34.

7. "Quote of the Day," accessed September 22, 2011, http://www.theteliosgroup.com/quotes/category/vision.
8. Aubrey Malphurs, "Sharpening the Focus of Your Vision," *Ministry Advantage* (July/Aug 1994): 1, 4.
9. Ibid., 4.
10. David Shibley, "Healthy Church Vision," *Ministries Today Institute* (September/October 2000): 46.
11. "Quotes," accessed September 24, 2011, http://www.shalomindia.com/quotes.php.
12. Smith, 33.
13. Alan Nelson, "Vision," *Rev!* (Jan/Feb 2006): 49.
14. Smith, 36.
15. Charles R. Swindoll, *Living Above the Level of Mediocrity: A Commitment to Excellence* (Waco, Tex: Word, 1987), 79–80.

Chapter 4

1. Andy Stanley, *Visioneering: God's Blueprint for Developing and Maintaining Vision* (Sister, Ore.: Multnomah, 1999), 202.
2. Gary L. McIntosh, "Biblical Planning," *Growth Points* (September 2009): 1.
3. Cited in "Reflections," *Christianity Today*, July 15, 1996, accessed September 27, 2011, http://www.christianitytoday.com/ct/1996/july15/ 6t8051.html.
4. "Henry David Thoreau," accessed September 27, 2011, http://www.quotationspage.com/quote/1598.html.
5. "Jim Rohn," accessed September 27, 2011, http://getmotivation.com/rohn.htm.
6. "Bobby Knight," accessed October 1, 2011, http://www.brainyquote.com/quotes/authors/b/bobby_knight.html.
7. Gordon MacDonald, *The Life God Blesses: Weathering the Storms of Life That Threaten the Soul* (Nashville: Thomas Nelson, 1994), 65–66.
8. Jim Rohn, "Creating Your Character Is Like an Artist Creating a Sculpture," (blog), accessed November 21, 2011, http://house-of-olifiers.com/sourcing-blog/2011/03/08/creating-your-character-articles-by-jim-rohn/.
9. Jim Collins, *Good to Great: Why Some Companies Make the Leap . . . and Others Don't* (New York: Harper Business, 2001), 41.
10. Ibid., 42.

Chapter 5

1. Robert F. Mager, "Fable of the Seahorse," accessed October 4, 2011, http://www.universallifestiles.com/Fable_of_the_Seahorse2.pdf.
2. Zig Ziglar, *Over the Top* (Nashville: Thomas Nelson, 1994), 160ff.
3. Ibid., 183.
4. "The Power of Ambition," accessed October 10, 2011, http://www.mindofsuccess.com/jim-rohn-quotes-the-power-of-ambition-part-4.html.
5. "Paul J. Meyer," accessed October 10, 2011, http://thinkexist.com/quotation/whatever_you_vividly_imagine-ardently_desire/253395.html.
6. Leith Anderson, "Looking to the Future," *Mastering Church Management* (Portland, Ore.: Multnomah, 1990), 69.
7. "Henry David Thoreau," accessed October 10, 2011, http://www.quotationspage.com/quote/3097.html.
8. "Napoleon Hill," accessed October 11, 2011, http://www.brainyquote.com/quotes/quotes/n/napoleonhi152852.html.
9. Stephen Strang, "Set Deadlines for Your Dreams," *New Man* (September/October 2000): 17.
10. Ziglar, 217–218.
11. Peter Drucker, *The Effective Executive: The Definitive Guide to Getting the Right Things Done* (New York: Harper & Row, 1967), 72.
12. "The Ultimate Reason to Become a Millionaire," accessed October 12, 2011, http://www.successmethods.org/mike_litman-a54.html.
13. Hans Finzel, *The Top Ten Mistakes Leaders Make* (Wheaton, Ill.: Victor Books, 1994), 193.
14. Cited by John Maxwell, *Developing the Leaders Around You: How to Help Others Reach Their Full Potential* (Nashville: Thomas Nelson, 1995), 95.
15. Robert Schuller, *You Can Become the Person You Want to Be* (New York: Hawthorn, 1973), 4.
16. "Message to Writers," accessed October 12, 2011, http://www.starving-writers.com/.

Chapter 6

1. Cited by Tom McKee, "When You Do Have a Youth Pastor," accessed October 17, 2011, http://www.ctlibrary.com/lebooks/theleadershiplibrary/musicyouth/ldlib06-10.html#1.

2. Cited in Donald T. Phillips, *Lincoln on Leadership: Executive Strategies for Tough Times* (New York: Warner Books, 1992), xv.
3. John C. Maxwell, "Security or Sabotage?," *INJOY Life Club*, vol. 14, no. (July 1998): 1.
4. Cited by Nancy Ortberg, "Ministry Team Diagnostics," *Leadership* (Spring 2008): 42.
5. Ibid., 43.
6. I am indebted to Leighton Ford for several of the ideas embodied in this section. See his chapter edited by George Barna: "Helping Leaders Grow," *Leaders on Leadership* (Ventura, Calif.: Regal, 1997), 128ff.
7. Ray Attiyah, "What Employees Expect of the 'Ideal' Supervisor," accessed October 20, 2011, http://www.bizjournals.com/cincinnati/stories/2003/03/10/smallb3.html.
8. "Dwight David Eisenhower," accessed October 23, 2011, http://thinkexist.com/quotes/dwight_david_eisenhower/.
9. Phillips, 18.
10. Ibid., 14.
11. J. Wilbur Chapman, "The Life & Work of Dwight Lyman Moody," accessed October 20, 2011, http://www.biblebelievers.com/moody/14.html.
12. Cited by David L. McKenna, *Power to Follow, Grace to Lead: Strategy for the Future of Christian Leadership* (Dallas, Tex.: Word, 1989), 102.
13. John Maxwell, *Developing the Leaders Around You: How to Help Others Reach Their Full Potential* (Nashville: Thomas Nelson, 1995), 172–173.
14. McKenna, 114.
15. Hans Finzel, *The Top Ten Mistakes Leaders Make* (Wheaton, Ill.: Victor Books, 1994), 84.
16. "Dwight D. Eisenhower," accessed October 23, 2011, http://www.brainyquote.com/quotes/quotes/d/dwightdei101562.html.
17. Cited in Phillips, 39.
18. Ibid., 39–40.
19. J. Oswald Sanders, *Spiritual Leadership: Principles of Excellence for Every Believer* (Chicago: Moody, 1967), 156.
20. Ibid., 167.
21. Cited in Phillips, 95.

22. "Diane Sawyer," accessed October 23, 2011, http://thinkexist.com/quotes/diane_sawyer/.
23. "Demand Low for Eisenhower Tapes," *Manhattan Mercury*, Tuesday, November 27, 1997, A3.
24. Max DePree, *Leadership Jazz* (New York: Crown Business, 1992), 1–2.

Chapter 7

1. Andy Stanley, *Visioneering: God's Blueprint for Developing and Maintaining Vision* (Sisters, Ore.: Multnomah, 1999), 89.
2. "Coaching and Leadership Quotations," accessed October 27, 2011, http://www.hoopsu.com/coaching-leadership-quotations.
3. Gary L. McIntosh, *Growth Points* (September 2009): 1.
4. Tom Mullins, *The Confidence Factor: The Key to Developing the Winning Edge for Life* (Nashville: Thomas Nelson, 2006), 82.
5. Cited in Herb Miller, "Accomplishing Worthy Goals: Being Smart is Not Enough!" *The Parish Paper* (February 2011): 1.
6. Tim Stafford, "Can We Talk?," *Christianity Today*, October 2, 1995, 32.
7. "Richard DeVos," accessed October 30, 2011, http://www.1-famous-quotes.com/quote/18050.
8. "Conductor Skitch Henderson dies at age 87," *USA Today*, November 2, 1995, accessed October 30, 2011, http://www.usatoday.com/life/people/2005-11-02-skitch-henderson-obit_x.html.
9. Hans Finzel, *The Top Ten Mistakes Leader Make* (Wheaton, Ill: Victor Books, 1994), 131.

Chapter 8

1. Paul J. Meyer, *The Dynamics of Personal Leadership* (Waco, Tex: Success Motivation Institute, Inc., 1969), 166–167.
2. Robert E. Logan and Sherilyn Carlton, *Coaching 101: Discover the Power of Coaching* (St. Charles, Ill.: ChurchSmart Resources, 2003), 16.
3. Linda Miller, "Counselor or Coach?" *Rev!*, September/October 2003, 56.
4. Ibid., 58.
5. Don Shula and Ken Blanchard, *Everyone's a Coach: You Can Inspire Anyone to Be a Winner* (Grand Rapids, Mich: Zondervan, 1995), 73.

6. "Johann Wolfgang Von Goethe," accessed November 6, 2011, http://www.englishforums.com/English/JohannWolfgangGoetheTreat/lnxxw/post.htm.
7. Logan and Carlton, 29.
8. "Anthony Robbins," accessed November 6, 2011, http://www.brainyquote.com/quotes/quotes/t/tonyrobbin132550.html.
9. "Oak Beams, New College Oxford," accessed November 5, 2011, http://atlasobscura.com/place/oak-beams-new-college-oxford.

Chapter 9

1. Cited in David Carter, "Your One Sustainable Competitive Advantage," accessed November 7, 2011, http://carterreport.scramjetstrategies. com/e_article001559864.cfm?x=b11,0,w.
2. Patrick Lencioni, *The Five Dysfunctions of a Team: A Leadership Fable* (San Francisco: Jossey-Bass, 2002), 188.
3. Cited in Max Lucado, *He Still Moves Stones* (Dallas, Tex.: Word, 1993), 91.
4. Jill Rosenfeld, "It's About Time," Fast Company, accessed March 1, 2012, http://www.fastcompany.com/magazine/29/one.html?page=0%2C4.
5. John Maxwell, *One Hour with God: Weekly Plan for Spiritual Growth* (El Cajon, Calif.: INJOY, 1994), 137.
6. Cited in Carson Pue, "Attracting and Developing Future Leaders," accessed November 10, 2011, http://www.christianleadershipalliance.org/?page=attractingleaders.
7. Tom Verducci, "Solitary Man," accessed November 10, 2011, http://sportsillustrated.cnn.com/vault/article/magazine/MAG1138188/index.htm.
8. Cited in Dominic Sama, "Conductor Arturo Toscanini Honored With A New Stamp," accessed November 10, 2011, http://articles.chicagotribune.com/1989-03-26/entertainment/8903300014_1_la-scala-silver-haired-conductor-new-stamp.

Chapter 10

1. Jo Anne Lyon, "Affirmation is a Choice," *Light from the Word* (February 29, 1996).

2. "Benjamin Franklin," accessed November 18, 2011, http://www.freefictionbooks.org/books/b/43485-benjamin-franklin-self-revealed-volume-i-of-2?start=186.
3. Lee Strobel, *God's Outrageous Claims: Thirteen Discoveries That Can Revolutionize Your Life* (Grand Rapids, Mich.: Zondervan, 1997), 133.
4. John Maxwell and Jim Dornan, *Becoming a Person of Influence: How to Positively Impact the Lives of Others* (Nashville: Thomas Nelson, 1997), 166.
5. Stan Toler, *Pastor's Little Instruction Book* (Nashville: Brentwood Music Publishing, 1963), 98.
6. "Positive Inspirational Quotes," accessed November 17, 2001, http://www.agiftofinspiration.com.au/quotes/inspirational.shtml.
7. Fred Smith, *Learning to Lead: Bringing Out the Best in People*, vol. 5, *The Leadership Library* (Waco, Tex.: Word, 1986), 83–84.
8. Tom Mullins, *The Confidence Factor: The Key to Developing the Winning Edge in Life* (Nashville: Thomas Nelson, 2006), 83–84.
9. "Leo F. Buscaglia," accessed November 17, 2011, http://thinkexist.com/quotation/too_often_we_underestimate_the_power_of_a_touch-a/213531.html.
10. "Friendship and Loyalty," accessed November 20, 2011, http://www.rawfoodinfo.com/articles/qte_friendship.html.
11. Patsy Clairmont, *Normal is Just a Setting on Your Dryer* (Wheaton, Ill.: Tyndale, 1999), cover.
12. "Co-dependent families and the roles we play in them," accessed November 20, 2011, http://brendamarroyauthor.wordpress.com/2011/09/05/co-dependent-families-and-the-roles-we-play-in-them/.
13. Cited in Ken Blanchard and Don Shula, *Everyone's a Coach: You Can Inspire Anyone to Be a Winner* (Grand Rapids, Mich: Zondervan, 1995). 129.
14. Hans Finzel, *The Top Ten Mistakes Leaders Make* (Wheaton, Ill.: Victor Books, 1994), 59.
15. Mary Ann Bird, "A Whisper Heard by the Heart," *PLUS* (Aug/Sept 2010): 27–28.